In Short
A Concise Guide to Good Writing

In Short

A Concise Guide to Good Writing

Louis I. Middleman

Virginia Polytechnic Institute and State University

St. Martin's Press   *New York*

Library of Congress Cataloging in Publication Data

Middleman, Louis I
  In short.

  1. English language—Rhetoric.   I. Title.
PE1408.M54   808'.042   80–29017
ISBN 0–312–41164–2

ACKNOWLEDGMENTS

From *On Philosophical Style* by Brand Blanshard (Bloomington: Indiana University Press, 1954). Originally published by Manchester University Press, Manchester, England, and reprinted with their permission.

From "To Err is Human," "Notes on Punctuation," and "Why Montaigne Is Not a Bore" in *The Medusa and the Snail* by Lewis Thomas. Copyright © 1974–1979 by Lewis Thomas. Originally appeared in The New England Journal of Medicine. Reprinted by permission of Viking Penguin Inc.

From "Lies, Lies, Lies" by Anthony Brandt. Copyright © 1977 by The Atlantic Monthly Company, Boston, Mass. Reprinted by permission of International Creative Management as agents for Anthony Brandt.

For my mother and father

Preface

Most students attempt to succeed in English Composition by asking or guessing what the instructor wants, then trying to provide it. How, I wondered, could I answer students' questions so as to bring out their best efforts—writing that reflects a genuine engagement with finding and shaping ideas—rather than encourage them to play safe, to retreat, self-shackled, into mere correctness? But "anything goes" is as unsatisfactory a first principle for good writing as rigid adherence to a set of prescriptions.

I believe that there is a way of guiding the writing process with a small set of ideas which, once understood, will appear obvious and natural. First is the plain fact that writing is usually addressed to someone else and must, therefore, take into account the audience's willingness and ability to receive it. Second, although we use words and other symbols to communicate, we want to communicate not words, but meaning, and to the extent that our symbols call attention to themselves *as* symbols, they may impede the reader's understanding.

This small book is meant not as a substitute for a comprehensive volume on rhetoric, grammar, and mechanics, but as a complement to such a text, designed to present in a few pages the chief concerns of a writer sending a message to a reader. The first chapter treats the relation between writer and audience, including the case of instructor-as-audience. The remainder focuses on the more particular matters of generating ideas, drafting, editing, and revising—all of which in reality take place concurrently and are "stages" only figuratively—and concludes with an introduction to writing the research paper.

An author's name on the title page of a book must always, I think, be an instance of synecdoche. It is certainly so in my case, standing for the many people whose encouragement, intelligence, and skill these acknowledgments make explicit.

Had Peter Phelps, formerly of St. Martin's Press, not asked early in 1977, "What are *you* working on these days, Louis?" I might never have completed even my prospectus. The project developed under the firm but genial scrutiny of St. Martin's editors Tom Broadbent and Nancy Perry and profited from the comments and suggestions of anonymous but much-heeded reviewers.

To my constant friend and former office mate at Harrisburg Area Community College, Michael A. Dockery, I owe the fruits of many hours' discussion about the teaching of writing. To Ann Heidbreder Eastman, Arthur M. Eastman, Timothy L.

Keegan, and Raymond L. Manganelli of Virginia Polytechnic Institute and State University and to Karen Melton, I am grateful for many hours of encouragement and close scrutiny at every stage of the manuscript's preparation. They always told me exactly what they thought, even when I winced.

Finally, I thank my students, whose hits and misses generated this little book and whose reports of its potential usefulness kept me at it.

Louis I. Middleman

Contents

In Short
A Concise Guide to Good Writing

Chapter 1

The Eight-and-a-Half-
by-Eleven High-Potency
Writing Tablet

Imagine on your head a stiff, yellow, cardboard hat in the shape of an equilateral triangle three feet on a side, with a bunch of green grapes dangling from each vertex. Why should you imagine such a thing? Well, but you have probably already done so, and that's the point: you couldn't help it. And just as my words influenced you, your words influence your reader. This central fact is the kernel of everything that follows.

When someone reads what you write, he or she is in your power. The trick, then, is to use that power effectively. Most readers stop if they become bored or annoyed, but teachers of writing are committed to peruse everything their students submit. Therefore, you must try to give them no choice but to enjoy it! This goal will be easier to reach if you enjoy the work also. I hope you will be motivated, partly from outside but mostly from within yourself, to compose what genuinely engages your attention and excitement. The biggest mistake you as a writer can make is to refrain from writing what and how you want to because of deciding in advance, and for no good reason, that the reader won't like it.

The Student and the Course: Assumptions and Goals

Chances are that you have entered your college writing course already aware of certain strengths and weaknesses. As the result of both directed and undirected practice, you should noticeably improve your performance as the year progresses. But don't expect to become perfect in two or three ten- to fifteen-week periods, and don't get discouraged about this. You have had many years of practice in spoken English, at the rate of thousands of words a day; the ratio of your oral practice to practice in writing is probably on the order of a million to one—even if you regularly leave notes on the refrigerator. Because you are not likely to be asked to write more than about five thousand words of prose in one term, which is an average of about fifty words a day, weekends and holidays included, you will need to spend a good deal of quiet time studying how to make those words count. You will write and rewrite and rerewrite. "Everything comes out wrong with me at first," said the American psychologist and philosopher William James, "but when [it is] once objectified in a crude shape, I can torture and poke and scrape and pat it till it offends me no more."[1]

The purpose of "Comp" is to help you learn how to convert mental events into written messages, and for this enterprise to succeed, you must take an active, willing part. In this and subsequent chapters I propose to do my part, which is not to make the writing process easy (it is not), but to make it less confusing by directing your energies along focused paths from the generation of ideas through to their polished final presentation.

More Power to You

Perhaps you have thought that the flow of authority in a writing class runs, and runs only, from instructor to student. In certain obvious ways this is true: the instructor selects the readings and texts, schedules assignments from them, establishes the number and sometimes the kind of papers and tests, and grades your work according to certain criteria.[2] But true *author*ity is yours; everything submitted for your instructor's response and evaluation is in your control. Every grin, smile, twinkle, or chortle; every brow-wrinkle, sigh, groan, grimace, or grunt called forth by your performance will be largely the result of your use of language.

---

[1]Quoted in Brand Blanshard, *On Philosophical Style* (Bloomington: Indiana University Press, 1954), p. 42.
[2]Remember that *criteria* is plural; the singular is *criterion*. Recall also that *phenomena* is plural and *phenomenon* singular. But watch out: two or more *data*, yes, but one *datum*. Can you add to this list?

At an early age, probably between one and two, you taught yourself to use and understand language as a more-or-less-agreed-upon set of symbols plus rules for combining them. This system enables you to formulate, send, and receive messages that determine or influence your own and others' thoughts, feelings, and actions. Consider now this simple interchange:

Waiter: "Coffee?"
Patron: "Yes. Cream and two sugars."

In only six words, two people have negotiated an arrangement with perfect clarity.

As the preceding example suggests, language use is normally intentional, purposeful, and restricted to a specific set of circumstances. We talk or write to ourselves and others to achieve some goal. You may recall the old joke about the chicken who crosses the road . . . to get to the other side. Let us inquire into some possible motives of this chicken. Is she hungry, and does she expect to find food? Is she being pursued by a hatchet-bearing poultry processor or a frisky dog? Does she need a little exercise or just want a change of scenery, a new perspective on the world? Listen, is somebody paying her to make this trip? The point is that without some push or pull, the chicken goes nowhere—and neither do words. Messages are not random but designed, designed to *move* us, to relocate us physically and mentally in order to take us anywhere from Louisiana to laughter, from New Jersey to new insight. As you develop your ability to communicate in writing, you will become increasingly sensitive to the relationship between language and the physical and mental responses of your readers.

I ask you now to agree that you must take greater care with written messages than with spoken ones. In conversation, people can and usually do rely on visual and verbal cues from the listener (facial and vocal expressions of confusion, dismay, interest, delight) that signal the need to clarify, to supply additional information, and to answer objections—in short, to create a well-supported bridge of communication from one mind to another. This process of progressive clarification is so natural that you may never have perceived it as involving continuous mutual control. But consider the purpose of such words and phrases as "Hey!" "Huh?" "Really?" "He *didn't*," "Right," "Not in my house you won't!" These are examples of instantaneous feedback that lets you know—indeed compels you to know—the immediate effect you have on your audience.

When you write, however, your audience is usually not present (which is usually why you write in the first place) to help you. Therefore, *in your imagination, you must become your audience.* You must first try to calculate how someone else, with knowledge and experience different from yours, is likely to react to your message, then decide what he or she needs to be told so that you can be sure the message will be understood exactly as it is meant. How familiar is your audience with the subject? What, if anything, do you know that tells you how much can be taken for granted? You have probably had conversations with friends in which you wanted to share your excitement about, say, a new high-powered stereo amplifier, an elegant proof of the Pythagorean theorem, or a joke based on Einstein's concept of space-time—only to be frustrated because the other person needed to be taken back to "square one" before being able to show any precise interest, let alone joy. This problem of gaps between the contexts of a sender and a receiver is serious enough in face-to-face dialogue, but at least it is clear to both parties when such a gap appears. The writer must try to *predict* possible gaps and fill them *in advance*.

The audience's familiarity with your context, however, is by no means your only concern. The audience also has a certain working vocabulary, which is a direct measure of its general knowledge, and a set of beliefs, values, likes, and dislikes. These, too, must be taken into account. You will seldom be able to know the characteristics of your audience fully or certainly; but the closer you come, the greater will be your chance of designing appropriate, fitting messages. Indeed, because appropriate language is what suits an audience, it may be profitable for you to imagine not only what your audience knows and likes but also what it is *wearing*, in order to decide on the degree of formality or informality you should try for. Writing addressed to a tuxedo and top hat will differ from writing addressed to shorts and a T-shirt.

The most immediately responsive audience—and therefore the easiest one to address successfully—is oneself. We never talk or write to ourselves in any vocabulary but our own, we always know the context of such messages, and we know our own preferences. Communicating with ourselves is, in short, safe: we don't have to "watch our language" for fear of someone else's disapproval or misunderstanding. It is, therefore, dangerously easy to forget that an audience of others is . . . *other* and cannot see things from our point of view unless we verbally *move* him, her, or them *to* it. (This phrase, "point of view," is so often used to mean opinion or idea that you may not have realized that it implies a definite perceiver who perceives something definite from a definite location.) Your audience will always be in some respects like yourself and capable of receiving information as you are. But your audience will also always be unlike yourself in knowledge and temperament, and you must build a bridge of words to cross the gap.

EXERCISES

1. Write a diary entry, which no one else will ever see, describing an important recent emotional experience involving at least one other person. Then write the description as part of a letter to
   a. Your mother or father.
   b. Your best friend.
   c. Another (or the other) person involved.
2. Write an explanation of why the sky is blue (or how hailstones form or how an integrated circuit chip works or any other scientific or technical principle) to
   a. Yourself, as a study aid for an upcoming essay exam.
   b. A curious but not scientifically or technically versed friend whose vocabulary contains none of the specialized terms you may have used in the explanation you wrote for yourself.

3. Write short advertisements with the purpose of "selling yourself" to two or more of the following:
   a. A would-be romantic involvement, to remove the "would-be."
   b. A specific professor, to make him or her let you into an already full class a week after the term begins.
   c. "The people" (specify the group), to get elected as something (specify).
   d. A creature from another planet, to show what a wonderful thing the human body is.
4. Find in a textbook you are now using or have used a short passage that you did not at first understand but that you now do understand as a result of having asked questions or having read other accounts of the material. Rewrite the passage so that you would have understood it the first time.

The Instructor as Audience: What the Opening Opens

Granted, a bottle opener opens bottles; and a can opener, cans; garage door openers, season openers, and eye openers open doors, seasons, and eyes. So, the opening of a composition opens the composition, right? Yes, but what help is that? Instead, remember this: the opening of a composition *opens the reader.*

Think for a moment about your own reading habits. You pick up a book, magazine, or newspaper and begin to read. Do you find yourself responding, "Wonderful. More!"? Do you at least consent to put up with it? Or do you put it down? If the last, I give the reason as follows: unless a piece of writing opens you, you close it. You might decide as a matter of fairness to assume some of the responsibility yourself and say that you are "not receptive." You could also answer, "It doesn't appeal to me." That's perfect. To appeal means to call, and an appealing piece of writing . . . appeals. It may vary in tone from an angry shout to a seductive purr, but its invariable effect is to capture your attention.

I ask you now to imagine your instructor about to take up something you have written. There he or she is, sitting at a table or desk stacked with papers, and yours could be anywhere among them. What is his mood? That depends on what his universe happens to look like at the moment. Has he just read a brilliant paper, a mediocre paper, or the un-paper? Has she just come from supper, having eaten a delicious steak—or her fifth meatloaf sandwich (on stale bread) in two days? Has he just lost twenty dollars because a friend actually did quit smoking for a month, or did he retrieve the money after a better friend proved that the first friend lied?

The unarguable truth behind such examples is that your instructor, like you and me and everybody, arrives at each new moment of experience with *a set of expectations*, generated by the sum of who's who and what's what at that moment. And you cannot predict or influence how your reader feels at the precise instant he or she reaches for your composition. But once it's in his or her hands, he or she is, as it were, in yours. Here are two consequences of the preceding statement:

1. Your first sentence must provide transition from absolutely anything in this or any other world to the world of your paper.

2. Because your first sentence will generate your reader's expectations about everything that follows, work hard to make it fresh, lively, and specific. Psychologists have found that we tend to remember beginnings (and ends) more than middles.

EXERCISES

1. Here are some actual first sentences from student compositions on the subject "What people and events have significantly influenced your choice of career?" What expectations do the sentences generate about what will follow? Analyze and explain how these expectations are (or are not) set up. Then divide the sentences into three categories: acceptable as is, capable of being saved, and beyond repair—discard. Rewrite the sentences in category two, and discuss your groupings and your revised versions in class.

   a. The topic of this paper is to be the influences of a choice of a career.
   b. Several things have influenced my decision to enter the field of gerontology.
   c. The major influence over my choice of a career has to do with my value of money.
   d. I've been a licensed practical nurse (LPN) for the last seven years, and I've had enough.
   e. Choosing a career has dwelled on my mind for over a decade.
   f. At forty-three years of age, I find it hard to answer your question.
   g. The obvious first step in any analysis is to define the subject.
   h. "Scientists study the world as it is; engineers create the world that never was."
   i. Amid the coming of the hellish period of life called adolescence or "young adulthood," there comes the realization that in a few short years one is somewhat obligated to choose a career.

2. Compile a list of first sentences of articles in popular

magazines and in books in the "best-seller" department of your nearest bookstore. Which sentences
make you want to read further? Why? Bring your list
to class for discussion.

A Final Initial Word About Effective Writing

Two classes of adjectives describe "good" writing.
The first consists of words like *clear* and *coherent*,
which refer to qualities the reader is likely to
think about only when they are absent. Clear writing, like a clean, flat window, is a medium for
transferring information without distortion or in-
terference. Such clarity is neutral: what is com-
municated, though clear, may be false, ugly, or
boring as well as true, beautiful, or fascinating.
The same neutrality applies to coherence. Writing
is coherent when its parts fit together not ran-
domly but inevitably, forming a whole that is obvi-
ously some one thing and not just anything at all.
Clarity and coherence are thus matters of form;
they are necessary components of effective writing but insufficient to guarantee it. "People eat
tuna fish" is both clear (it says exactly what I want
it to) and coherent (its parts fit together in a definite way), but it is hardly exciting enough to be
nominated for Clause of the Year.

We use a different class of terms to describe the
effect that writing has on a reader—words such as
*fertile, thoughtful, original, persuasive, forceful,
impressive, compelling, striking,* and *incisive.* Notice that some of these terms imply a battle or a
contest; who or what, in those cases, is the adversary? *The adversary is the indifference of your*

reader. A writer needs to apply Newton's first law of motion, the law of inertia, which states that a body at rest will remain at rest, and a body in motion will continue to move in a straight line, unless acted upon by an external force. Hence my own first law of composition: Assuming that your reader is at best relaxed and at worst preoccupied or actively hostile, you must also assume that he or she will move from either position only if compelled to do so by the power of your words to engage, sustain, and reward attention.

The remainder of this book is devoted to helping you gain and command that power.

Chapter 2

The Overall Picture:
From Topic to Thesis to Draft

Prewriting: What's the Big Idea?

"A journey of a thousand miles begins with the first step," says an old Chinese proverb. True. But something must come before that step to set the traveler's path. In the same way, a message of a thousand pages (or two or fifty-eight) begins before the first word. What do you know or wish you knew? What do you want to say about it? To whom? How? Why? You really can't start writing until you have thought these questions through and arrived at answers that, though subject to change, at least give you the feeling that you know what to do next.

Finding the "what" is sometimes the hardest and most frustrating part of the writing process. When it is accomplished only after long and harum-scarum rummaging in and through our mental attics and pantries, not to mention basements, crannies, and nooks, we let out a sigh of relief and declare a short holiday. In many cases you will not be asked to devise your own "what" but to select one from a list provided by your instructor. To the extent that freedom of choice is a burden, you may welcome someone else's efforts at lifting it. Finally, however, the responsibility falls on you: the message must be uniquely yours.

It is no secret that your best writing will result from your best thinking, generated by involvement and engagement with some aspect of experience. Whether you are to pick your own writing topics "out of thin air" or to choose them from a mimeographed sheet, you await and desire the onset of *interest* and *curiosity*. The origins of these words provide clues about how to achieve the mental states they name. *Curiosity* comes from Latin *cūra* (care), whose meanings as a verb include "having a strong feeling or opinion" and "wishing," and as a noun, "distress and uncertainty."[1] *Interest* derives from two Latin words, *inter + esse*, "to be in between" (as opposed to being securely *here* or *there*). What emerges from these etymologies is the implication that your best writing will be the final product of what begins as puzzlement, bewilderment, amazement, a feeling of discord, discrepancy, tension, contradiction, confusion. In essence, something that bothers you, disturbs you, throws you off balance pleasantly or otherwise is likely to be a good starting point for thinking and writing that will challenge you to transform nonsense into sense, muddlement into understanding, disorder into pattern.

---

[1]For all definitions and word origins cited in this book, I consulted *The American Heritage Dictionary of the English Language* (Boston: Houghton Mifflin Company, 1978).

EXERCISE

List ten things that puzzle you. Then choose the two or three that you would most like to resolve, and explain why.

Are you uncertain how to proceed with this exercise? If so, here is a procedure to help you in the form of a series of questions. It's called a *heuristic* procedure, from a Greek word meaning "to discover" or "find." As I have no idea what items may be on your list of puzzlements, I shall use one from my own as an example: *olives.*

Heuristic Procedure

1. What word or phrase specifies the puzzle or its source? (Olives.)

2. What question specifies the nature of the puzzle? (Who "invented" the olive?)

3. What did you first experience or learn that created this specific puzzlement? (A few years ago I learned from a chemistry instructor friend that green olives fresh off the tree are poisonous and must be soaked in a potassium-salt solution before we can safely eat them.)

4. Why does this puzzle bother you? (First, I like olives and would like to express my retroactive thanks to the discoverer. Second—and this is the crux, or should I say the pimiento, of the matter—I am curious about what actually happened way back whenever. Was some unfortunate Greek, Hebrew, or Spanish lad or maiden found dead under an olive tree with the last lethal ovoid clenched between thumb, index finger, and teeth? Somehow or other the word got around: Don't eat olives off the tree! But who figured out how to befriend

this fruit? Did an ancient specimen from a coastal grove roll into the sea, soak, lose its toxicity, then wash ashore to meet its discoverer? If not this, what? Deliberate experiments to boil, fry, or bake the poison out?)

5. To whom or what have you gone for help, and with what results? (Books. No help, although I haven't completed my search yet.)

6. To whom or what *could* you go for help? (Other books, olive growers, food-processing companies.)

7. If different sources provide inconsistent or contradictory information, how can you decide which to believe? (I have as yet found *no* information, that is, nothing to reduce my initial uncertainty. That's why olives still head my bewilderment list. In general, however, the thing to do at this point is to go back to step one and put this *new* puzzle through the heuristic procedure.)

8. What solution, as far as you have been able to determine, exists? If none, can you show that no solution is possible? Or is it conceivable that some day you or someone else will discover it? (I can't prove that the edible olive's history is in principle unknowable, which gives me renewed hope that I or another may some day successfully pit him- or herself against this problem.)

9. How can you apply the solution you have found? That is, what difference does it make in the way you think, believe, feel, and act? Or, if no solution is available, how will you confront the puzzle or whatever part of it remains? By trying to forget it? Convincing yourself that it's not really so important? Making up a solution you like and that nobody can disprove? (I will continue to eat and

enjoy green olives, ignorant as I may remain of their true story.)

From "Oh, Oh!" to "Aha!"

The procedure just outlined should help you begin to generate interesting essays when you are permitted, encouraged, or required to choose your own topic and write about something that has *already* aroused your curiosity. Here is another method, which should be useful when your instructor demands an essay on a certain topic, say, "whales," and will accept nothing else. It is probably not possible to become enthusiastic about just anything, but what of that? Think positively; accept the subject as a bracing challenge to your intelligence.

Your task is, first, to discover the range of your potential responses to the topic, then to select the best, most interesting "Aha!" *Discovery* is the perfect word for this activity. It means *uncovering* what is in some sense already there, waiting in the labyrinth of a trillion brain cells for the skillful or lucky seeker. Now luck is wonderful, greatly to be prized, and welcome whenever it arrives—but it is not a sufficiently dependable basis for a method. Go for skill: give luck something to latch onto.

To begin explaining this second procedure, I define an "Aha!" as a suddenly perceived *connection* between two or more things that you did not previously see as connected. Like ions in solution, bits of experience wander about our minds, and sometimes, when they come together—bang!—we may find that something new, surprising, and strangely wonderful has occurred, as table salt, for example, results from the union of sodium and chlorine, a hyperactive metal and a poisonous gas.

Now to the method. You've got to write about whales? No help for it? ("Well, there *are* other topics on the list, all bummers, and this one's the best of the worst.") Okay. What you must be able to do is to formulate a question that in some way arouses your curiosity and interest and asks "Whales *what*?" or "What *about* whales?" The answer to this question will become your *thesis*, the leading idea for your essay. The thesis will satisfy the demand "Whales *what*?" by specifying the connections you will have perceived and subsequently intend to make clear to your reader. (By the way, if you have used the heuristic procedure in the previous section to explore a question, you have already practiced formulating a thesis, for a thesis is what the answer to question 8 produces: "What solution, as far as you have been able to determine, exists?" The essence of any solution is a *connection* between the source of the puzzle and what resolves it.)

It is necessary now for you to take inventory of your present knowledge about the topic. Make notes on paper—words and phrases are fine—of anything that you consider to be information about whales (or whatever). If you draw a blank or nearly a blank at this point, which may occur with a highly specialized topic, like "satyr plays," "mitochondria," or "eighteenth-century Italian violin varnishes," the thing to do is to learn something about your topic by spending a few hours in the library. Your mind won't be able to do any connecting unless it's stocked with potential connectors.

Before moving ahead to help you generate questions, I want to pause to stress the distinction between a topic and a thesis. A topic is *not* a thesis. Knowing your topic, you know what you will be writing *about*—whales, for example—but nothing more because "whales" is merely an area or field of possible thought and study, not an "Aha!" *Topic* comes from a Greek noun meaning "place," and *thesis* from a Greek verb meaning "to put into place" or "organize." So your topic is "where you go" to look for your thesis, and your thesis is "what you do when you get there" in order to make sense—your sense—of that place.

So: "whales" is not a thesis. How about "humpbacked whales"? No, that's just a smaller "place." "Jonah and the whale"? No again, for even though that phrase contains a connector-word, *and*, it gives no hint of the *kind* of connection that an essay on this topic might make. I must still ask, "Jonah and the whale *what*?" Here, by contrast, are some possible theses: "In spite of lobbying by numerous concerned groups around the world, the great whales may all have been killed before the middle of the next century"; "The humpbacked whale is the singer of a song so long and complex that scientists are only slowly beginning to fathom its mysterious beauty and purpose"; "Jonah could, as the Bible relates, have survived in the belly of the 'great fish' for three days and nights." Notice that whereas the topics—whales, humpbacked whales, and Jonah and the whale—are nouns or noun phrases, the theses generated from them are complete sentences, with subjects *and* predicates. The topics provide the subjects of the thesis sentences, and the predicates, with verbs and their objects, say something about the topics that specifies the nature of the connections to be developed in an essay. Concerning the last example of a thesis, notice that the *denial* of that assertion would make an equally acceptable basis for development: "Jonah could *not*, as the Bible relates, have survived. . . ." A thesis need not be absolutely, unequivocally true. It must only indicate clearly the kind of connection that a writer intends to make.

Now, how might you make some connections and begin to get curious about a topic? In a book called *The Necessary Angel*, twentieth-century American poet Wallace Stevens proposed something that happens to be extraordinarily useful for this purpose. In what could be called the fundamental theorem of poetry, Stevens suggested that the possibilities of metaphor are unlimited because everything is, in some way, like everything else.[2] Stevens's idea, really an idea-about-ideas, can be used to generate "Aha's" leading to theses in the following way. First, put "whales" and everything you know about them off to one side, and turn your full attention to making as complete a list as you can of the subjects and activities that interest you. Start from strength. Part of someone's list could look like this:

---

[2] A metaphor is an "Aha!" in which the perceived connection is expressed as an identity: Herbert is an oak; you're the cream in my coffee. EXERCISE: Notice, from your own speech and writing and those of others, how hard it is to use language for very long without falling into explicit or implied metaphor ("hard"? "falling"?). Reserve a notebook section for your observations. Metaphoric language can be found sleeping all over the place; wake it up.

> sex
> hunting
> cooking
> crime
> music
> religion
> painting
> money
> physics
> biology
> teeth
> mathematics
> racquetball

Now bring "whales" back, write it to the left of the list, and draw lines that connect it to each item. Get ready for more potential "Aha's" than you can shake a harpoon at. "Whales and crime," for example, could make you wonder about whale theft now or in the past. Who's doing (or did) it? What are (were) the penalties? "Whales and biology" could lead to the question, "If each of a whale's eyes sees something different, how does its brain reconcile and make sense out of the two images?" I could go on, but it will be better for you to do it yourself, with *your own interests* as the starting points.

EXERCISE

Make up your list, draw the lines, and for each connection try to formulate at least one question that specifies "Whales *what*?" If you use any of my items, good luck with *racquetball*—although "games whales play" may have possibilities. *Note:* For "whales" you may certainly substitute anything else, whether it be a topic assigned by your instructor or one of your own choosing.

From Thesis to Plan

Once you discover your thesis or anything that even begins to feel like one, write it down. (Please, write it down whenever and wherever it comes to you. If that's not possible, then do so as soon as you can. I personally have lost what seemed at the time marvels of insight because I told myself not to worry—I'd *never* forget anything *that* good. I wish I could provide an example.) Now give your thesis the "So what?" test. That is, say it aloud in as authoritative a tone as you can muster; then, playing the devil's advocate—in your imagination becoming your own severest audience—demand, "So what?" If you can't imagine arousing the curiosity and interest of a potential reader, go back to square two and suitably modify the thesis. If that doesn't work, generate more ideas until you find one that won't wilt or cringe under the pressure of such a question.

One property of a good thesis is that it suggests to both the writer and the reader the direction in which the rest of the paper will go. Because the thesis is your "point"—that is, it marks the point on the reader's mental map toward which you intend your essay to lead him or her—it contains, implicitly or explicitly, both the route to be followed and the sights along the way.[3] To put this

---

[3]*Explicit* and *implicit* come from a Latin root meaning "to fold." Something explicit is something *un*folded or folded *out*, whereas something implicit is still folded *in*. Have you ever temporarily lost a sock in the dryer because it got folded into a towel, sheet, or shirt? You know it's there, implicitly; if you're lucky, the first or second unfolding will make your knowledge as well as your sock explicit. (Some dryers, however, eat socks—though never whole pairs. It's a mystery.)

still another way, the thesis is the essay in embryo. You the writer, having conceived it, must now bring it to birth.

Essay, a word I have used synonymously with *message*, comes from a French word meaning "an attempt" or "try." An essay records a mental journey of discovery and self-discovery. As a writer you begin like a trailblazer, trying to find something, to make sense of something. The path of your first attempt is likely not to be straightforward, both because you may not know exactly where you're going and also because certain trails may turn out to be dead ends. Discovery is essentially a messy business for most of us, full of false starts, sudden clearings, and just as sudden overgrowths and pitfalls. Finally, however, you find the right track, you are sure of your destination, and you get there. It is then possible to backtrack and guide your reader with confidence and relative ease—as though the route and the goal (and any pleasant detours) were inevitable and you knew them all along.

An essay, in short, is an attempt first to arrive yourself at a certain understanding and then skillfully to move your reader to that same understanding. Understanding involves two kinds of information: objective information (facts and hypotheses) and subjective information (feelings, values, and attitudes). In order to select the elements of your essay, then, you must be able to answer these two questions:

1. What objective information do you want your reader to receive from your essay? That is, what do you want your reader to *know* or *know how to do* as a result of reading it?

2. What *attitude* toward this objective information do you want to create in your reader? In other words, how and to what degree (if any) do you want to *slant* your essay?

EXERCISE

Choose a thesis, perhaps one that you generated in the exercise on page 21. Then prepare to write an essay developing that thesis by answering the two preceding questions. The object of this exercise is to map out more fully the mental journey on which you intend to take your reader.

The plan you are now assembling may take the form of an outline that anyone could understand. It could also be a series of notes and phrases that are meaningless to anyone but you. Different writers work differently, and some prefer to do much of this planning in their heads, so that when the first paragraph meets paper, it serves as a kind of outline itself. But no matter how you proceed, *write down* your best ideas *as soon as they come to mind.* Don't let them get away.

From Plan to Draft

Well, it's about time to write an essay, don't you think? Are you ready? No? About 90 percent of the time, neither am I. In spite of my having probably written a great deal more than you—hundreds of essays since I was a freshman in college—and in spite of the helpful hints I've stumbled upon, read about, developed, practiced, and tried to pass on to you thus far, when I sit down, alone with an idea and a blank piece of paper, I'm nervous. I feel called upon to write something wonderful but fear that I'll produce instead something embarrassingly silly, trivial, or simply dull. As long as I can manage to put off writing, I'm safe. So I hear every sound as a possible knock on the door; I monitor every bodily sense for a dissatisfaction fulfillable only by my getting up from desk or table. Anything to evade the merciless criticism of that empty paper. What to do?

Just start. That's my only remedy. You have, of course, already started by generating a thesis and thinking about where you're going to go with it. Write the thesis down again, take a deep breath—and write another sentence. Keep going. The beauty of putting *anything* down on paper is that you give yourself *something* to work with. The mind works by association, so give it something to associate with. The mind also works by trial and error, and error literally means "wandering." So go ahead, and wander freely, making connections right and left *without worrying about being wrong.* *Wrong* originally meant "crooked"; William Blake wrote, "Improvement makes strait roads; but the crooked roads without Improvement are roads of Genius." Follow your genius, your generative faculty, and never doubt that you have one. Your mind is a deluxe model, equipped to do wonders as a matter of course. And perhaps the greatest wonder is that we all learn from mistakes. Lewis Thomas writes:

> Whenever new kinds of thinking are about to be accomplished, or new varieties of music, there has to be an argument beforehand. With two sides de-

bating in the same mind, haranguing, there is an amiable understanding that one is right and the other wrong. Sooner or later the thing is settled, but there can be no action at all if there are not the two sides, and the argument. The hope is in the faculty of wrongness, the tendency toward error. The capacity to leap across mountains of information to land lightly on the wrong side represents the highest of human endowments.[4]

In other words, a mistake or an "accident" will prove helpful either by directing you to what is right or by permitting you to discover something you would not have discovered by straightforward, error-free thinking.

Are the first sentences you write not the perfect way to begin? Don't worry: you can always change or abandon them later on. The first stage of a satellite-launching rocket drops off after thirty seconds or so; its purpose is to get the project going, to overcome tremendous inertia. And once your idea begins to take off, you may find that you can profitably discard your first stage, too. Also, don't be too concerned about spelling, mechanics, and perfect word choice while you're jotting ideas down or composing a first draft. The ideas and their arrangement are too important to be lost through undue attention to what at this stage is of minor concern. It's hard to think clearly in a swarm of gnats.

If your thesis is firm and you have arranged the parts of its development so as to be able to make your reader arrive where and how you wish, there is little more to be said here about your actual

[4]Lewis Thomas, *The Medusa and the Snail: More Notes of a Biology Watcher* (New York: The Viking Press, 1979), pp. 38–39.

composing process. But here's a tip. Some people write first drafts at one sitting; others require several. I suggest that, if you stop somewhere between the beginning and the end, you write yourself a note specifying as precisely as possible *what comes next*. Otherwise, when you sit down to write again, you may find that no amount of perspiration will bring back the original inspiration. Also, although you will probably have been assigned to write an essay of a certain length, you should not worry about fulfilling a word requirement, especially during this rough draft stage. You will often find that it takes more words to express yourself than you originally thought you would need. Writing, like speech, is linear—one word after another—and just as it often takes ten minutes to explain to a listener what comes to you in a (nonlinear) flash, it usually takes more space to translate a mental event into a written message than you at first supposed.

And here are two final hints. Try, even while composing your first draft, to keep the parts of your essay harmoniously balanced. If you are describing the best and the worst hamburger you ever ate, don't write three pages about one and three sentences about the other. Next, remember to make what is important and outstanding in your mind important and outstanding in your essay. Often a writer will neglect to develop what he or she finds most significant about an idea or an event simply because what is clear and compelling at the sender's end appears too obvious to mention. Remember that your reader is someone else, someone who does not know your mind until you make it available through your sentences and paragraphs.

Testing Your Draft for Coherent Organization

May I offer congratulations on the accomplishment of your first draft? It feels good—doesn't it?—to know that in some sense the piece is *there*, down on paper, under your control. As to the parts that may still bother you, recall that William James could "torture and poke and scrape and pat," and so can you. Take a break and relax. (Unless it's 3 A.M. and the final copy is due in five hours; in that case, turn immediately to the last section of chapter 5, on revision. But next time give yourself more breathing space.) Then, unless the draft came out in a lovely, unblotted flourish, copy it over so that you can see more clearly what you have done. Next, starting at the beginning and working through to the end, read each paragraph and figure out, in as few words as possible, the question it answers. List these questions in order on a separate sheet. Finished? You have just constructed an outline of your essay, which you can use to detect any major structural flaws. With your list in front of you, ask the following:

1. Is there a paragraph that simply doesn't answer anything? If so, should it be eliminated as pure waste, or is there a way to revise it so that it does answer a question implied by your thesis?
2. Is there a paragraph that "promises" answers your essay does not provide? Either fulfill the promise or remove the paragraph.
3. Is there a paragraph that answers two or more distinct questions, so that you should think about splitting the paragraph up?
4. Do you answer the same question in more than one

paragraph? If so, should you eliminate one of the paragraphs or combine the two?

5. Finally, do the questions now follow one another in a logical order? That is, will a reader be ready for the answer to question 7 after 6 after 5, and so on, or does he or she need the answer to question 8 before the answer to question 4 makes sense?

Using this procedure to criticize your first draft will enable you to arrive at a series of questions, each finally standing for one paragraph, that in sum constitute the outline of a coherent essay. And you will find that when the parts are arranged in the proper sequence, moving from one to the next will present few, if any, problems. It is easy and natural to make smooth connections between elements that fit—just as it is difficult and frustrating to yoke together pieces that don't.

Postscript

Although a writer often does proceed step by step from topic to thesis to draft, the process is not always as straightforward as this chapter makes it seem. Even the part about the essential messiness of discovery makes the act of composition seem a good deal tidier than it usually is.

So what I want to say here is this: It is just as likely that your thesis will grow out of your first draft as that your first draft will grow out of your thesis. Yes, you start from something; and yes, it's a great help to begin from a clear central idea. But if along the way you find something even better because a new connection abruptly presents itself and you *see*—"*That's* what I'm driving at!"—then by all means develop the new insight. In short, you may often not realize exactly where you're going until you stumble into it and are suddenly there. Don't let any one person's "writing method" prevent you from using and enjoying all your powers of discovery.

Chapter 3

Back Those Points: Support Your Local Generalization

Writing with Point

When we are asked what points are made in a piece of writing, we answer with statements variously called generalizations, abstractions, or conclusions. A *point*, then, is a condensation, an essence to which particulars boil down. The "Aha!" that produced the draft you have just tested for coherence is the main point of that essay, and the answers to the questions you pulled from each of the essay's paragraphs are the subsidiary points that elaborate, clarify, and refine the main point.

Permit me to illustrate this view of point as an actual point, the vertex of an angle. The converging lines in the figure on the next page suggest the writer's need to guide the reader within the boundaries of a given thought; anything beside or not to the point is . . . pointless.

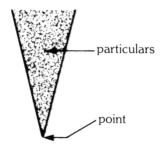

In order to "make your points" and to impress them upon your reader, you must back them with the specifics, the details that led you to assert those points in the first place. When we say that writing is "impressive" or "makes an impression," we are using figurative language. Literally, an impression is a mark left in something relatively softer by something relatively harder. If you want your reader to respond to your points, to share your perceptions, you must recreate for him or her the mental events that gave rise to those perceptions in you.

A writer's need to be specific is partly explained by the fact that all common nouns are abstractions and refer to general entities. Take, for example, *chair*. *Chair* is a convenient package used to refer to the common properties of a large number of particular items: armchairs, swivel chairs, folding chairs, wheelchairs, reclining chairs, electric chairs, Morris chairs, rocking chairs, and so on. The word *chair* is really the name of a category or a class—chair-ness or chair-hood. When we hear or see the word *chair*, we *may* respond by imagining a particular one, or we may not. If as writers we want to create an image of a high-backed, late-Victorian, dinner-table chair with claw feet and a green brocade seat, then *chair* by itself just won't do the job. For in the real world there is no "general" chair; you have never sat in, bumped against, or bought one.

The preceding example may be broadened to yield the following statement: There is no such thing as a general event. *Nothing happens in general.* It's convenient to talk and write as if general events did exist—in general, one might say, a banana dropped Monday noon from a height of five feet will hit the ground before Tuesday. Fine. But no one has ever seen, let alone dropped, a general banana onto a general piece of the planet. We *conclude* that a dropped banana falls because of a large number of similar—but individual, particular—events that converge to yield the generalization "Near the earth, dropped bananas fall rapidly." Because nothing happens in general, you must not write generalizations and expect your reader to infer the pertinent details.

To write with point, to write impressively, is to use enough of the particulars that led you to your conclusions to capture your reader's attention and focus it on those particulars. He or she may then actively follow the process by which you reached your conclusions and thereby be moved to share them. Professor Blanshard admirably says:

> Most men's minds are so constituted that they have to think by means of examples; if you do not supply these, they will supply them for themselves, and if you leave it wholly to them, they will do it badly. On the other hand, if you start from familiar things, they are very quick to make the necessary generalizations. In a sense they are making such generalizations constantly; whenever they recog-

nize the thing before them as a chair or a lamp-post, they are leaping from the particular to the general by a process of implicit classification.[1]

EXERCISE

Go back over the essay you wrote for chapter 2—or any piece of your writing, really—and on a separate sheet of paper write down the "points" that support the thesis. Then, to decide where you have written impressively and where you have not, ask the following questions about each point:

1. Do I believe this?
2. What specific details lead me to conclude that it is true?
3. Have I put those details into my essay, so that a reader can reach the same conclusions in the same way I did?

If you *don't* believe a certain point, you should probably not make it—unless your purpose is to deceive! If pertinent details are missing, supply them if you can. And in case you know that your supporting details are, by themselves, too weak or insufficient to make a point you nevertheless believe, indicate to the reader the "hunchy" or hypothetical or intuitive status of the point.

Writing as a Process of Discrimination and Selection

The American novelist Henry James once made the following distinction between life and art. Life, wrote James, is "all inclusion and confu-

[1]Brand Blanshard, *On Philosophical Style* (Bloomington: Indiana University Press, 1954), p. 32.

sion," whereas art is all "discrimination and selection." To say that life is "inclusion" is to observe
that our physical existence proceeds along continuous lines from "now" to "then" and from "here"
to "there." The child who complains on December
23 of being unable to wait for Christmas may well
receive the sobering reply: "Herbert, you have no
choice." And life is "confusion" because so many
more events occur to and around us than we can
possibly predict and prepare for. Why does Aunt
Ethel telephone while I'm in the shower? Out of
perversity? Probably not: she simply doesn't know
I'm there. Imagine any crowded scene—a major
airport the day before Thanksgiving or a morning
rush hour traffic-and-people jam in New York,
Houston, or San Francisco—and you will get a vivid picture of life as "inclusion and confusion."

Art, on the other hand, is "discrimination and
selection," *and the same terms apply to writing.*
The artist, the writer, looking at the mental and
physical experiences and events we call life,
makes two major and related decisions in order to
shape a message for an audience:

1. Not everything is equally significant. (discrimination)
2. Not everything available can be used. (selection)

Life is presented to us; it is simply there, an undif-
ferentiated aggregate, inclusive and confused.
When we re-present it in writing, we must choose
from all of the material at hand the particular set
of details that will make our message clear, not
confused, and exclusively what we wish, omitting
what is not significant or pertinent to our purpose
and our audience.

EXERCISES

1. List twenty things you saw or experienced yesterday. Then imagine you are writing an autobiography. Which of the twenty would you include and exclude from it, and why?
2. Carefully reread the most recent essay you have written. For each detail that you supplied, decide why you included it and why you excluded others you might have used. Then make any additions or deletions that seem appropriate.

Enough or Too Much?

How do you decide what is enough illustration and what is too much? The answer depends on your purpose in sending a particular message to a particular audience. The word *specific* comes through Latin from an Indo-European root meaning "to observe," "see," or "look at." To decide how specific you need to be, then, is to realize that *whatever you want your reader to see, you must show him or her.* This principle seems obvious, and in a sense it is. But notice that we commonly use the word *see* to mean much more than "perceive visually." Indeed, we often say, "I see" when it is not literally a matter of seeing at all. Thus, the original statement about specificity may be recast as follows: Whatever you want your reader to understand, perceive, apprehend, or take in, you must present in a form that he or she is adequate to receive.

Your reader, in short, cannot read your mind directly. You, the writer, must permit him or her to read your mind indirectly by first reading it directly yourself and then translating that reading into marks on paper. As discussed in chapter 1, it is usually not possible to know your reader's adequateness with absolute certainty. For this reason, sending a message is always something of an experiment. What you *can* do with certainty is to take inventory of the thoughts, feelings, and images that are present in your own mind as you conceive your message, then see to it that the most important of these are explicitly present in the message you finally send.

What else can you do? Seek the advice and criticism of readers whose knowledge, intelligence, and judgment you respect, people who can be counted on to play the devil's advocate with your entire essay as you earlier did yourself while you were formulating your thesis. Your instructor will, I trust, be *one* of these sensitive and helpful critics, but he or she should not be the only one—and preferably not even the first. Henry David Thoreau wrote in *Walden*, "Those things for which the most money is demanded are never the things which the student most wants. Tuition, for instance, is an important item in the term bill, while for the far more valuable education which he gets by associating with the most cultivated of his contemporaries no charge is made." Use this free resource freely; show your work to friends first, and only then to strangers.

A Word on Balance

Although there is no formula for the proper balance between generalizations and specifics, it is

possible to get a feeling for what's right by thinking in terms of panoramic shots and close-ups in
films. Notice how a skillful filmmaker prepares
for a scene with a wide-angle image, then focuses
on the particular aspect to be considered in detail.
A movie made up exclusively of distance shots
would frustrate any viewer, who would soon begin
saying, "Well? Well!?" An unrelieved sequence of
close-ups would be similarly annoying; the viewer
will demand that the individual images contribute
to some overall effect.

So, as you read over what you write, pay attention to where you are providing a wide-angle shot
and where you are coming in close. Try to keep
your audience from leaving the theater.

Chapter 4

Style

Style and Styles

We commonly use the word *style* in many ways that have nothing to do with writing. There are hairstyles, learning styles, life-styles; styles of architecture, of clothing, furniture, cars, music, print, painting, pitching, dance, management, cooking, and many others. The question may then be put: Having a style, what is it that each of these has? According to *The American Heritage Dictionary*, the word *style* derives from Latin *stilus*, a sharp, pointed instrument used for writing, marking, or engraving. A style, then, is a distinctive set of definite, marked, recognizable features.

What produces a writer's style? Does a writer have a style in the way he or she has fingerprints, which no amount of tampering can fully disguise? Or does a writer select and use different styles as different audiences and purposes demand? The answer is both. A writer's style is the product of an individual personality interacting with the world; it is the result of how a writer characteristically makes sense of things. Your style, then, is the sum of things you cannot change—who you are, what you know—plus all the deliberate, conscious choices you make in the process of writing. This book is not about what you are, but about the choices you as a writer make. For our purposes, then, the best definition of *style* may be the one given by the philosopher-mathematician Alfred North Whitehead in *The Aims of Education* (1929): "Style is the direct attainment of a foreseen end, simply and without waste."

Information and Noise

According to a branch of inquiry known as "information theory," *information* is defined as *the reduction of uncertainty*, and anything that interferes with this reduction is called *noise*. This theory, which embraces all conceivable systems for the coding, sending, and receiving of messages—involving not only print and voice but also light and electronic impulses—is highly technical and mathematical, but its application to writing simply and without waste is straightforward. The careful stylist puts information in and leaves noise out. Information informs, but noise annoys.

When I was in twelfth grade, I walked into my English class one morning and was startled to see the normally blank front slate shouting infinitive imperatives—"To be omitted from all writing: *very, really, rather, somewhat, quite, the fact that, due to the fact that.*" The lesson for the day was Style; I remember only the words on the board and the idea that style was a matter of what you *left out*. Until that morning I had innocently supposed that style was something you *put in*. It is both, of course, but let's concentrate now on style as skillful omission.

What's the matter with words like *really, very*, and so on? My teacher asked that they be omitted because, she said, they were usually not helpful in transmitting something from one mind to another. Does the sentence "Herbert said he really had a very delicious meal" convey any more information than "Herbert said he had a delicious meal"? No; in this case, my teacher was right. The first sentence is noisy. How about "I'm blue due to the fact that it's raining"? All right: "I'm blue because it's raining." As Henry David Thoreau wrote in *Walden*, "Simplify, simplify."

EXERCISE

From your own reading in newspapers, textbooks, and so forth, collect a dozen sentences containing the "to be omitted" words and phrases, and write them down. In which sentences are the words and phrases noise, and in which are they genuinely informative? Bring your list to class for discussion. (Are there other noisy words and phrases to be added to the Probably Omit list? Which ones? Collect some examples of these, too.)

Repetition: Noisy or Informative?

We often repeat on purpose—and for a good reason: to emphasize. Thoreau appears not to have taken his own advice when he repeated *simplify*, but the two are just right. The second is for emphasis and rhythm, which one alone doesn't carry. Style is not *merely* a matter of leaving out. Here for another example is the opening line from the play *Saint Joan* by George Bernard Shaw. The speaker is a local squire, Baudricourt, who is mystified at the behavior of his chickens as reported by the steward: "No eggs! No eggs!! Thousand thunders, man, what do you mean by no eggs?" It is possible to shorten this outburst to yield "No eggs? Thousand thunders, man, what do you mean?" (Before reading the next sentence, please say the two versions aloud and with as much theatricality as you can manage. Okay?) I hope you found Shaw's original much more effective. Eliminate what appears to be noise, and you eliminate the very soul of the utterance. Those extra eggs were not absentmindedly added on; Shaw consciously and deliberately built them in.

EXERCISE

Below are two well-known sentences, one from Lincoln's "Gettysburg Address" and the other a translation from Caesar's *Gallic Wars*—and two versions shortened by the deletion of repeated words. Note and discuss the differences.

We cannot dedicate—we cannot consecrate—we cannot hallow—this ground.

We cannot dedicate, consecrate, or hallow this ground.

I came; I saw; I conquered.

I came, saw, and conquered.

Repetition produces emphasis. *Warning: repetition produces emphasis whether you want it to or not.* To repeat deliberately in order to add force to your words is one thing. But to repeat words and phrases unintentionally either emphasizes the unimportant or dulls the important by overinsistence, with the result that what you wanted to highlight fades. In such cases, more is less, as in the following sentence: "I tried to answer the phone, but the phone was too far away; and by the time I reached the phone, the phone had stopped ringing." When a reader starts seeing words instead of meaning, repetition has gone too far. It is not enough to call such extra freight *unnecessary*, a term that suggests a merely harmless addition. The reader can't help but process the noise as well as the information; and the more energy spent getting nowhere, the less there is for understanding and responding to the message.

There is another kind of repetition to avoid—that in which a word is used in two different ways and momentarily confuses the sense of the message. In an essay about how to advertise an electric car, I read: "The first ad concerned the performance of the Zoom. I selected an auto enthusiast to perform the tests." Unless I miss my guess, the second *perform* disturbed you a bit because it clashes with the word's first use. Initially, the *car* is performing; then suddenly the *driver* is. This awkward repetition can be easily corrected by replacing *perform* in the second sentence with *conduct* or *do*.

In order to test a piece of writing for unwanted repetitions, read it slowly and

1. Circle or underline every instance of a repeated word or phrase. Often just seeing the repetitions is the hardest part. You'd have sworn they weren't there when you read your work quickly; that's because you were reading for meaning—which you understood easily because it's *your* meaning—and didn't actually see the words themselves at all.

2. When in doubt, factor. This motto, prominently displayed above the front board in my high school algebra class, applies also to writing. Noisy repetitions of *subjects* or *verbs* can be factored out like algebraic terms: $sv_1 + sv_2 = s(v_1 + v_2)$, and $s_1v + s_2v = (s_1 + s_2)v$. In English, "Herbert came in and Herbert sat down" becomes "Herbert came in and sat down," and "Herbert came in and Sally came in" becomes "Herbert and Sally came in." Prepositional phrases are also candidates for factoring: "Herbert was coming into the room as Sally was going out ø̸f̸ ̸t̸h̸ǿ ̸r̸ǿǿm̸." An essay on the importance of reading contained the sentence, "This is not to say that reading is the only way of obtaining knowledge because we can also obtain knowledge through watching and listening." That's a good thought, but it could have been factored to make a better sentence: "This is not to say that reading is the only way of obtaining knowledge because we can also do it through watching and listening."

3. Remove as much repetitive noise as you can.

Wordiness

Wordiness is a word that is often used by many people to express the idea that something that was written by someone in a larger number of words could have been expressed in a smaller number of words. That is, *wordiness* means using more words than necessary. It's bad manners to make a reader plow through the thirty-eight words of the first sentence when the second's seven do the trick. How to get from the first version to the second? We can start by finding repetitions:

> *Wordiness* is a word that is often used by many people to express the idea that something that was written by someone *in a* larger *number of* words could have been expressed *in a* smaller *number of* words.

The noise from express – expressed is the result of an awkward repetition; the other noise comes from emphasizing the unimportant. Starting with is – is, we see that we can't remove the first one; but what about the second? Yes, if that goes too, as it surely can. So can the third that if we also remove the *was*. The result:

> a. *Wordiness* is a word often used by many people to express the idea that something written by someone in a larger number of words could have been *conveyed* [to remove the awkwardness] in a smaller number of words.

Four down, twenty-six to go. All right—*wordiness* is a word; does anybody need to be told *that*? It's a word used by many people. (By what else? Dogs?) Written *by* someone. Well, that's no information, for, of course, it didn't write itself. And let's factor out the second *of words*. Our next intermediate version is

b. *Wordiness* is often used to express the idea that something written in a larger number of words could have been conveyed in a smaller number.

We're making progress. Now, isn't there a word often used to express the idea "often used to express the idea"? Yes: "means." What about "larger number of" and "smaller number ~~of~~"? *More* and *fewer* (not *less*, which is used to refer to *amount*). So,

c. *Wordiness* means that something written in more words could have been conveyed in fewer.

To take it from here is to realize that a *more . . . than* construction is possible and that *something written* is expendable because it doesn't refer to anything more specific than *words.* Thus,

d. *Wordiness* means using more words than necessary.

Done. Or are we? Why stop now, when we're doing so well? "More than necessary" means "too many," so

e. *Wordiness* means using too many words.

What are you to learn from this long shortening?

1. From *a* you see that it is often possible to remove words like *that is, that was, who are,* and so forth. Here are some additional examples:

The man ~~who is~~ coming this way is Herbert.

Herbert and Sally were the only people ~~who were~~ not eating liver.

The noise ~~that~~ the firecracker made is one ~~that~~ I'll never forget.

The book ~~that is~~ on the table is the best ~~that~~ I've read.

2. From *b* you understand that what is obvious is needless to say; common examples are ~~free~~ gift and ~~added~~ bonus.

3. From *c* you learn that a word may take the place of its definition. Instead of saying that a ball rolls down an inclined surface such that a straight line joining any two points on the surface lies wholly in the surface, you say the ball rolls down an inclined *plane*. A related idea is that clauses and prepositional phrases can often be shortened to adjectives: "the book that is heavy" becomes "the heavy book"; "the meadow that is covered with grass" becomes "the grassy meadow"; and "the chart for testing how well someone can see" becomes "the eye chart."

4. In the movement from *c* to *d* you observe that sometimes it is necessary not merely to subtract but to recast. The general rule is to give your sentences "exercise and a diet." That takes some insight, which takes practice. The sentence on reading, dealt with in the preceding section, can be still further improved: "This is not to say that reading is the only way to learn; we can also watch and listen."

5. From *e* you realize that where to stop is a matter of personal style. I could have cut the sentence down to four words—*Wordiness* means excessive verbiage—but that sounds stilted to me.

EXERCISE

Remove noise from the following paragraph, which may be titled "The Convenience of Being Reasonable."

I am of the belief that I have omitted to put in a mention of the fact that, in the very first of the ship voyages that I took from the city of Boston, being quite becalmed in the boat when the boat was in the waters off an island that was called Block Island, our people on the boat set themselves about the labor of bringing cod out of the water and up into the boat, and they really did haul up a very great many of those cod. Hitherto I had stuck to that resolution which I had about not eating the flesh of animals for food, and on this occasion I considered, right along with my master, who was named Tyron, the taking of every finny creature as really a kind of murder for which the creatures themselves really gave no provocation, since not a single one of them had, or ever could do to us any harmful injury that might in some way make the slaughter a just thing. All this seemed very reasonable. But I had in a former time been a great lover of that particular kind of food, and, when this came in a heated state out of the pan in which it was fried, it smelled an admirably good smell. I sort of balanced for rather some time in the middle between the principle at issue and my inclination to eat it, till I recollected the fact that, at the time when the fish were opened by those on board, I was able to observe smaller creatures of the same kind taken right out of their stomachs; at that point the thought occurred to me, "If you eat one another, I don't really see the reason why it is that we mayn't eat you, too." So I then dined upon cod very heartily, and I continued to eat in the company of other people, returning only now and then occasionally to a diet exclusively made up of vegetables. So convenient a thing it is to be a *reasonable creature*, because it enables one to find or make a reason for everything that one has a mind to do.[1]

[1]This paragraph of 366 words is corrupted from Benjamin Franklin's *Autobiography*, in which it takes 203. After you have worked on the version above, you might enjoy comparing your result with the original. (You may even prefer some of your own choices to his.)

Clichés

Accidental repetitions frustrate the reader and weaken your message because they create noise instead of providing information. A *cliché* is a phrase—like "good as gold" or "gentle as a lamb"—that has been dulled by repetition, not within individual sentences or paragraphs, but across the writings of many people. The noun *cliché* originally was (and still is) a printer's term, the past participle of the French verb *clicher*, to *stereotype*, which means to join words frequently used together into a single mold, die, or stamp in order to save the typesetter the labor of making them over and over "from scratch." How many times would you, as the printer of a small-town newspaper that's still set in movable type, compose p-r-o-b-a-b-i-l-i-t-y–o-f–p-r-e-c-i-p-i-t-a-t-i-o-n character by character before deciding, "Hey, this is silly!"? If necessity is the mother of invention, then laziness is at least a first cousin.

The reason to avoid clichés comes from the very ease of repeating them: at both the sender's and the receiver's ends they lessen the need to think. What's good for the typesetter, who is a compositor of words as *words*, is bad for the writer, a composer of words as *meaning*. A reader is always busy predicting what's coming next in order to reduce uncertainty and to derive understanding. But if the features of a message are completely predictable, the reader stops paying attention.

Many clichés began as figures of speech, for example, "spur of the moment" (implied metaphor: the moment is a horse) and "This is (or is not) my cup of tea," and served the worthy purpose of focusing and increasing attention. But when too much of a good thing isn't nipped in the bud, everything goes to wrack and ruin. What started out fresh as a daisy becomes dull as dishwater. At this point in time, let me ask you, straight from the shoulder: is it not sheer folly, by and large, to let clichés rain cats and dogs?

The problem is that what is a cliché to one person may not be to another; it depends on what different people have heard and read. You will best learn what is acceptable and not acceptable to various audiences the same way you learned language years ago—by paying attention to the effects your words produce and modifying them accordingly. You will also do well to avoid expressions you *know* to be trite from having heard them or seen them in print time and . . . er, often. Clichés may on occasion be deliberately twisted in order to create a striking or amusing effect. Write "a horse of a different color," and you will raise no eyebrows. But "a horse of a different texture" will startle the reader into participation by violating his or her prediction of what's coming next. A student writing about E. B. White's *Charlotte's Web*, a cherished book from her childhood, used this tactic beautifully when she observed that Charlotte the spider's love and friendship for insecure Wilbur the pig finally gave him the confidence "to stand on his own four feet."

EXERCISES

1. Make as long a list as you can of expressions you consider to be clichés. Identify those whose status as clichés seems open to doubt. Compare your list with the lists of your classmates, and see if they agree with your judgments. After class discussion, some-

one might want to collect and collate the lists and provide everyone with a copy.
2. Play with any items on your or someone else's list, deliberately twisting them for effect.

Choppiness

The human mind quickly seizes on patterns of all kinds in making sense of the world. A writer must, therefore, try to avoid unintentionally creating patterns that will distract the reader's attention from the message. Such distracting patterns may occur *within* sentences—for example, as the result of clichés and noisy repetitions. But sentences themselves can create a distracting repetitive pattern called choppiness. More than two or three successive sentences of similar length, structure, and rhythm are likely—unless the effect is deliberate, emphatic—to engage the reader's mind in predicting the *shape* of the next one and straying from the *sense.* Concerning sentence length as it relates to choppiness, I can do no better than to quote from Professor Blanshard:

> If one is to have any rule about this, it must, I think, be a vague one, to the effect that each sentence should carry the thought one step forward. But what is to count as one step? A sentence at its simplest makes one statement, but if we were to make only one statement per sentence, our writing would be unbearable. "Sir John came out of his house. He was in morning dress. He wore a top hat. He wore a monocle. He wore spats. He carried a cane. He hailed a taxi." Intolerable! When details all hang together to make one picture, they can be grasped without difficulty as forming a single unit, and we throw them together into one sentence: "Sir John, radiant in morning dress, with top hat,

monocle, spats, and cane, emerged from his door
and hailed a taxi." But in regions of difficulty, it is
a test of literary tact to know and take into account
the length of the reader's stride. The ideal is a row
of stepping-stones just far enough apart to enable
him to keep moving without compelling him to
make hops, skips, and jumps, still less leaps in the
dark.[2]

Lincoln was mistaken at Gettysburg when he
said that "The world will little note, nor long remember, what we say here. . . ." His "Gettysburg
Address" is perhaps the best-remembered speech
in American history. He might, however, have suc-
ceeded in writing a forgettable speech had he be-
gun choppily, like this: "Four score and seven
years ago, our fathers did something. They
brought forth a new nation. The nation was on this
continent. It was a nation conceived in liberty. It
was a nation dedicated to a proposition. The
proposition was that all men are created equal."
Are you tired yet?

EXERCISES

1. Use the complete text of Lincoln's address, which
   follows, or find another short piece of prose that you
   especially like, and "ruin" the whole thing by recast-
   ing it as a series of choppy sentences. Include all the
   information, but make it as tedious to read as possible. Keep this deliberately botched version handy
   when you're trying to write well, as a kind of *memen-
   to mori* (a Latin phrase which has come to mean "re-
   minder of death"; in the present case perhaps *me-
   mento bori* is more apt).

[2]Brand Blanshard, *On Philosophical Style* (Bloomington: Indiana University Press, 1954), pp. 51–52.

Four score and seven years ago our fathers brought forth on this continent a new nation, conceived in liberty, and dedicated to the proposition that all men are created equal. Now we are engaged in a great civil war, testing whether that nation, or any nation so conceived and so dedicated, can long endure. We are met on a great battlefield of that war. We have come to dedicate a portion of that field, as a final resting place for those who here gave their lives that that nation might live. It is altogether fitting and proper that we should do this. But, in a larger sense, we can not dedicate—we can not consecrate—we can not hallow—this ground. The brave men, living and dead, who struggled here, have consecrated it, far above our poor power to add or detract. The world will little note, nor long remember, what we say here, but it can never forget what they did here. It is for us the living, rather, to be dedicated here to the unfinished work which they who fought here have thus far so nobly advanced. It is rather for us to be here dedicated to the great task remaining before us—that from these honored dead we take increased devotion to that cause for which they gave the last full measure of devotion—that we here highly resolve that these dead shall not have died in vain—that this nation, under God, shall have a new birth of freedom—and that government of the people, by the people, for the people, shall not perish from the earth.

2. If you would like a lot of practice in varying the lengths and patterns of sentences, ask your instructor to suggest a text on "sentence combining." Such a book will give lists of choppy "kernel" sentences to put together, like the following:

    There was a beginning.

    At that time, God created something.

    He created two things.

One thing was the heaven.

The other thing was the earth.

Combine these kernels into one sentence.

Rhythm and Emphasis

How will you decide the best way to combine the kernel sentences above? Some choices are

1. God, in the beginning, created the heaven and the earth.

2. God created, in the beginning, the heaven and the earth.

3. God created the heaven and the earth in the beginning.

4. The heaven and the earth were created by God in the beginning.

5. The heaven and the earth were created in the beginning by God.

6. In the beginning, the heaven and the earth were created by God.

7. In the beginning, God created the heaven and the earth.

I hope you find it as refreshing as I do to come at last to the King James version. What is so *right* about that arrangement? What does it have that the others don't? We can reject 4, 5, and 6, the passive constructions, because they emphasize *what was done* at the expense of *who did it*.[3] Such em-

---

[3] A passive construction, or instance of "passive voice," is formed from the verb *to be* plus a past participle. In the preceding sentence, *is formed* is in the passive voice, which is used

phasis is the main feature of the passive voice, which is appropriate when you deliberately want to play down or omit the doer or when you don't know who or what the doer is. *God* should not assume a minor role in the sentence under consideration. Arrangement 1 does put *God* emphatically up front, but it contains three roadblocks (what three?) between subject and verb, resulting in a harsh, start-stop-start-stop rhythm. Version 2 unpleasantly separates the verb from the direct object. And version 3 gets my "nay" vote because it seems to end twice, the prepositional phrase "in the beginning" behaving like a tail on an animal that isn't supposed to have one. Version 7 is the best because it puts everything where it belongs: the linear arrangement of words and pauses follows the unfolding of meaning. As Professor Blanshard says, "The rule is to make the emphases of sense and rhythm coincide. Plain men know by a sort of instinct where to hit hard; they never say, 'There is in my mind a desire which would be gratified if you were to transfer the hammer into my possession'; they say, 'Give me the hammer'" (*On Philosophical Style*, p. 57).

EXERCISE

Find a newspaper report of a recent event that interests you, and underline the instances of passive voice. Which ones seem to reflect the writer's conscious attempt to focus on the thing done as opposed to the do-

---

to emphasize the *object* of the action rather than the agent. The opposite of passive voice is *active voice*, which puts the agent up front—*I wrote* this sentence—as opposed to highlighting *what* I wrote in the passive version—*This sentence was written by me.*

er? Which ones apparently proceed from no such moti-
vation, so that the active voice is preferable?

Fragments Yes and No

A fragment is either a subordinate clause all by itself (for example, "If Herbert liked liver.") or,
more generally, a word or a group of words that
lacks—or appears to lack—a subject or a verb or
both. Got that? Yes? No? Those last three questions express complete thoughts *elliptically*, that
is, with words absent from the page but present to
a reader's understanding: (Have you) got that? Yes
(you have)? No (you haven't)? Elliptical fragments
are common in speech because the risk of misunderstanding is matched by the ease with which the
speaker can *see* if the listener is puzzled and can
clarify, if necessary. And certainly we don't need
to talk to ourselves in complete sentences. In formal writing, however, fragments should be saved
for special occasions when you want to break the
rhythm for a particular emphatic effect, to startle
or amuse. Enough.

   Enough, that is, for *deliberate* fragments. It is
one thing to know that your reader will automati-
cally supply what is needed when your words
don't physically represent the whole message, but
it is something else to get lost in a long sentence
when, having written enough words to become
confused about main and subordinate clauses,
about grammatical subjects and verbs. You stop
too soon. In the terms of Blanshard's stepping-
stone analogy, such an accidental fragment has
the effect of removing the next stone just as the
reader is about to land on it. Splash.

What's the Good Word?

Promote Nouns and Verbs

What would you do if all adjectives and adverbs suddenly went away? I, for one, would have had to think harder about how to put the preceding sentence and might have written, "Suppose adjectives and adverbs vanished." Could we get along with only nouns and verbs? (Would nouns and verbs suffice?) No. We need words that distinguish *when, why, where, how,* and *what kind.* "A medium-rare, 1½-inch porterhouse steak served hot off the charcoal" contains precisely the qualifications I like. With only nouns and verbs, how could I order in a restaurant? "Bring meat"? And to the question "Is supper ready?" the answer "No" might be correct, but it's not as helpful as "Almost." Nevertheless, we experience life primarily as a series of events in which subjects act upon objects; that is, we are primarily aware of *things* and *processes,* nouns and verbs. Writing should not obscure these basic elements by burying them in paraphrases full of unnecessary words.

Here are some tips on promoting nouns and verbs.

1. When you can, combine a noun and a qualifying clause or prepositional phrase into a single noun, so that "leader of the committee" becomes "chairperson," and "entry way into a building," "vestibule." Now here are some for you to try: person coming in first in a race; book that has been read and loved for a long time; prod given by releasing the index finger, which has been bent so that its tip presses against the thumb (hint: the word begins with *fi*); tree that doesn't lose its

leaves in the winter; strip running along the outside edge of a highway; person who writes poems; person passionately devoted to a cause.

2. You can also try to find a single, lean verb to replace a bulkier verb phrase—"make use of" becomes "use," and "think carefully about" becomes "ponder" or "weigh." Can you find single-verb equivalents for the following: look closely at; come to the conclusion that; hit over and over; keep something going over a period of time; put an end to; put an emphasis on; stop suddenly and refuse to continue? (Only you can prevent yourself from writing, "Only you can take steps toward seeing to it that bulky verb phrases don't occur.")

3. Once you have drafted a piece of writing, read it over, reconsider its adjectives and adverbs, and delete those that contribute neither precision nor flair. Beware of vague words like the following, which can easily give a sentence the "blahs": *great, good, bad, real(ly), fine, interesting*, and *nice*.[4]

4. In short, don't qualify a statement to death; be bold. Instead of writing, "I frequently have a persistent, tender feeling for you which leads me to the conclusion that for now, at any rate, I am in that more or less pleasant bondage called love. May I in any way be informed as to the extent to which this exquisite sentiment is in prospect of being reciprocated?" write, "I love you. Do you love me?" But don't let my advice prevent you from using the *right* qualifiers when they count. It would be terrible to have to answer, when asked how you wanted your porterhouse steak cooked, "I'm not allowed to say." Adjectives and adverbs can produce powerful effects, as you will notice in a mo-

---

[4]*Nice* used to mean "exquisitely precise," but now refers to . . . er . . . what? Anyhow, have an exquisitely precise day.

ment when you imagine the difference between hot buttered popcorn and cold buttered popcorn.

EXERCISES

1. Find and bring to class for discussion five magazine advertisements for products you would like to own. Circle the nouns and verbs and underline the adjectives and adverbs. How have the writers of these advertisements used words to draw your attention and incite your desire to buy? What would the advertisements lose without the qualifiers?

2. Write down as many advertising slogans as you can think of—for fast-food restaurants, beverages, political or ecological campaigns, airlines, you name it—and discuss the relative importance and specific effects of nouns, verbs, and qualifiers. (I once spent ten minutes on the phone with a marketing agency interviewer who wanted to know what I thought of *friendly* as the word to describe the kind of skies flown by a certain company. I told her it was perfect; the rest is history.)

3. Bring to class for discussion a descriptive passage from a book, magazine, or newspaper that you find especially brilliant because of the qualifiers its author chose. You might even prepare a handout of the passage with the qualifiers left blank, ask your colleagues to experiment with filling them in, and discuss the results.

Vocabulary as Treasure: The Dictionary as a Recreation Area

In the eleventh-century English epic *Beowulf*, embattled heroes prepare themselves for powerful speech by reaching into their *word-hoards*, and modern German preserves the metaphor in *Wortschatz*, literally "word-treasury." If wealth is potential, then vocabulary is a kind of wealth; and the bigger our treasury, the more we have to draw on in order to say, understand, and think—and by these actions control our lives.[5]

Have you ever been with a child who has just learned a new word? For him or her it is a treasure indeed, performing strong magic, commanding attention and action: "Hungry!" We would do well to emulate the child's appetite for new words. Having learned one, we start to find it "all over the place." Actually it's been there all along; only we weren't. Looking up words takes time, yes, but the dividends make the investment sound.

My advice is to keep the dictionary handy—at hand—when you read and use it regularly, not for *every* unfamiliar word, perhaps, but certainly for those that you can't figure out from the context. Probably a good 95 percent of the words you know you learned without looking them up. But occasionally, especially when you're reading something unfamiliar, you encounter words that make the context itself unclear. Such a passage may well seem more like noise than information because your mind isn't stored with enough connectors to grasp it. Some examples of context-confusing words from my own experience are italicized in the following sentences:

Take the second right after the *tarn*.

Most of us have a higher tolerance for *paranomasia* than we would like to admit.

He gave me a *fillip* to get me going.

[5]For a fascinating discussion of the control and obliteration of free thought through the reduction of vocabulary, see "The Principles of Newspeak," the appendix to George Orwell's *1984*.

The second right after the *what*? It could be anything, but it happens to be a mountain lake. *Paranomasia*, I learned from the dictionary, is a fancy word for *punning*, and *fillip* is the forefinger prod you may not have needed on page 57, in case you've already looked it up.

My next advice is that when you look a word up, you study the *etymology*, which is likely to help you remember the meaning. Take, for example, the adjective *desultory*. I must have looked this word up fifteen times before its meaning sank in permanently, and the reason for the delay was that I neglected its roots. The word means "moving or jumping from one thing to another"; that *sult* says "jump!" Perfect. The etymology gives a vivid image to the phrase "desultory reading." And if you happen to own *The American Heritage Dictionary*, you can turn to the appendix of Indo-European roots and learn that other members of this word family include *sauté, salient, somersault, result, exult, insult*, and . . . *salmon* (the leaping fish).

One more example. While writing about *emphasis* earlier in this chapter, I realized I had no idea how the word came to indicate "something that receives a lot of attention." So I looked it up and found its Indo-European root to be "shine," and among its relatives *beacon, beckon, photograph, phantasm, berry* (bright-colored fruit), and *banner*. How about that! To emphasize is to shine a light upon or wave a flag. What wonderful amusement to page desultorily through the dictionary (*amuse* comes from a root meaning "to sniff around") on the scent of discoveries.

Let me add, however, a note of caution. Some of

the words you learn by playing in the dictionary you may have to keep under your hat, so to speak, because to use them might appear pretentious. Once, on the way to *protocol*, I stumbled upon *monopsony*, defined as "a market situation in which the product or service of several sellers is sought by only one buyer." But although the word means something simple enough, and has for me a beautiful sound—sort of like the name of a Greek goddess—I've never been able to use it in a piece of writing. Until now! Still, I'm glad to have it in my treasury. Neurophysiologists affirm that no matter how much I remember, billions of brain cells are bound to go unused during my lifetime. So, as I've got plenty, I'll not worry about reserving a few for *monopsony*.

Suggestions

1. Set aside a notebook for your word-hoard, and make deposits regularly. Include definitions, origins, and family members.
2. Once a week, open your dictionary to a page at random, scan the words, and study those that interest you. You will find yourself exclaiming "Oh, so *that's* what _____ means!" often enough to keep you going.

Some Questions and Answers

At the beginning of a writing course I invite my students to submit anonymous questions, the answers to which they think will help them get to know me as an audience. Most questions request information about *style*, that is, about what they may feel free to *put in* and what they should *leave out*. The written answers help us both, giving them less to worry about and me less to repeat. Here are some of the most frequently asked questions and my answers.[6] (Your own instructor may answer them differently: Find out!)

Q: *Will you accept "you" instead of "one"?*

A: "One," though frequent in French (*on*), German (*man*) and other languages to express a generalized impersonal subject, singular or plural, sometimes sounds stilted in English, and "you" is the substitute. "One does what one must" is correct but quite formal; "you do what you have to" is more appropriate in an informal context. I object to "you" in two cases: when in a paragraph or over several paragraphs "you" is mixed for no apparent reason with another personal pronoun, and when no pronoun at all is required, as in "(You) Take a right at Chestnut, and (you) swing into the first driveway on your left." In general, ask yourself if your're you-ing for a particular purpose, for instance, to address the reader directly or achieve some effect not possible any other way.

Q: *How many sentences do you expect in a paragraph?*

A: I expect as many or as few as you need (one needs?) to get the job done. Sometimes there will be *no* sentences in a paragraph if by sentence you mean a subject-verb combination. A single word like *Perhaps* or a deliberate fragment could, in the proper circumstances, exquisitely jolt the reader both visually and psychologically. If your question

---

[6]These questions and answers, as well as the pair in the next chapter, appeared in slightly different form in "Psych-Out Q's and A's," *ADE Bulletin*, No. 63 (February 1980), 39–43.

means, "Do you especially like or dislike long or short paragraphs (and how long is *long*; how short is *short*)?" then I answer that several one- or two-sentence paragraphs in a row usually indicate that the writer either doesn't have enough to say about a set of points or that he or she has failed to combine ideas that belong together. *Indent* literally means "put a toothmark into"; to begin a paragraph, then, is to take a mental bite. Depending on what and how much you bite at a given time, you must do more or less chewing. To test a paragraph, state the question the paragraph is designed to answer; then decide whether it says enough to satisfy your audience or more than enough to tire him, her, or them.

A final suggestion: Vary the length and pattern of your sentences and paragraphs. *Any* form repeated too many times will put the reader to sleep.

Q: *Do you prefer us to use long words instead of just our basic vocabulary?*

A: No. Use a long word only where a short one won't do. Question: Is *syzygy* shorter or longer than *Mississippi*? Both, eh? Well, *perambulate* is surely longer than *walk*. Eschew pretentious lexicality. Words inserted just to impress me usually don't, especially because they almost always stick out like a sore apposable digit. You will know when you have made a word your own and can use it comfortably.

Q: *Are you more concerned with the length of a paper or with the quality? Do you like a lot of B.S.?*

A: With the quality. And NO. I define B.S. as waste material unwillingly but deliberately added to fulfill a word requirement. Don't do it. It's silly and a poor use of time, yours and mine. But please don't refrain from supplying adequate detail to flesh out your points even if you must write *more* than I ask for. You'll know when you're padding and when not, and so will I. Word limits are set to give a rough idea of what's expected; if I didn't tell you in advance approximately how much to write, you'd ask me. The proper length for an essay depends on the purpose to be accomplished.

Q: *Is it acceptable to use "etc."?*

A: *Etc.*, short for Latin *et cetera* ("and the rest"), should be used only when the reader can be assumed to know what "the rest" is. Example: "Herbert wrote the first hundred thousand cardinal numbers in lipstick on the newly painted yellow wall: 1, 2, 3, etc." Please do not use *etc.* to try to make a reader think you could go on and on with fine and pertinent examples when, in fact, the two you give are *it*. Further, *never* use *and etc.*, which would mean "and and the rest."

Q: *How do you feel about split infinitives? Are they taboo or just a minor grammatical error?*

A: The rule against splitting infinitives comes from eighteenth-century grammarians' desire to base English grammar on Latin, which they considered the most "perfect" language. (Grammar books were best-sellers in those days, as a relatively unlettered rising industrial class sought to write and speak the King's English, thereby to add the polish of gentility to their new wealth.) There is no *to* in Latin infinitives; infinitive stems simply have certain endings. So, reasoned these grammarians, what Latin hath joined let no Englishman put asunder—and bingo, there's the rule. Obey it when you like the sound and rhythm it produces or when you're writing for an audience that demands adherence. I usually do not split infinitives, but to utterly prohibit them seems antiquated.

Q: *Is there anything wrong with using the words* I think, I feel, I believe *when we're writing our opinions?*

A: Usually you don't need such words. Because it is you who writes, it must be you who thinks, feels, or believes. Sometimes a writer wishes not to make a definite statement, worrying that if he or she does so, a reader holding a different opinion will blast it. So the writer tries to soften the blow with *I think* or *I feel* or *I believe.* That strategy doesn't impress me: I can still ask *why* someone thinks, feels, or believes in a certain way. Therefore, provide the bases for your opinions. Plato makes Socrates say that opinion is something between ignorance and knowledge. That's a fine definition. The closer to knowledge an opinion is, the better—and the easier to support.

It is, however, legitimate to use those expressions to refer to a genuine uncertainty—one the reader will perceive to be such. Examples: "I think I left the gas burner on, but I'm not sure." "I believe Aunt Ethel's coming home; I see a car that looks like hers." "I feel that I should go to the party because I said I would, but I don't really want to."

Q: *When is this chapter going to end?*
A: Now. Onward!

Chapter 5

Taking Care: Punctuation, Usage, Spelling, Neatness, and Revision

We write to communicate meaning, not words. The marks we make on paper (or on walls, telephone poles, sidewalks, the sky) are translations of something in our heads into symbols that represent what we want to create in the mind of someone else. This someone else, the reader, must perform a second translation, from words and other symbols back into meaning. Much of the translation process is mysterious: no one knows just how the brain produces and stores meaning.[1] It is clear, however, that a writer can accidentally or deliberately obstruct the reader's ability to under-

[1] For a highly readable account of what *is* known, see Frank Smith, *Comprehension and Learning* (New York: Holt, Rinehart and Winston, 1975). The idea of the two translations I take from E. F. Schumacher, *A Guide for the Perplexed* (New York: Harper & Row, 1977), p. 81.

stand a written message. A reader continuously predicts what's coming next on the basis of what he or she already knows about how language works generally and about the specific context of the message. Thus, when everything seems to be going smoothly, a reader is stopped and momentarily annoyed at the unpleasant surprise that suddenly sentence of rest the immediately sense the make doesn't. mean See? I what

Every competent user of English is able, as you were, to figure out the correct arrangement of the fifteen symbols at the end of the previous paragraph. No one knows precisely how you did *that* either, and in case you don't think it was any great feat, consider that those fifteen symbols could have been arranged in 1,307,674,300,000 different ways. It probably took you only a few seconds to choose the proper one. Pretty good, eh?

Very well: we are all experts, geniuses at finding meaningful patterns of words and punctuation marks, but we are nonetheless bothered when our prediction of what's coming next is totally incorrect. We don't like to have to pay attention to symbols *as* symbols for even a few seconds—unless we are *expecting* a joke or a verbal problem. Consider the following sentence: "Because of recent breakthroughs in the development of inexpensive and durable plastic people will be able to afford furniture and appliances that they could not if such items were fashioned from wood or metal." Plastic people, already? Let us hope not. The writer omitted an important comma in the fashioning of this sentence, one without which the intended message is temporarily lost.

A writer strives for mechanical perfection, as the preceding example suggests, not so that the reader will notice it but, on the contrary, precisely so that the reader will *not* notice. A student asked me, "When grading a paper, what do you concern yourself with the most? Grammar, or content and originality?" I answered:

> When eating a piece of cake, I concern myself with the taste and texture; I don't think about or respond to the flour *as* flour unless I'm forced to do so by finding an unmixed lump of it suddenly gumming up my mouth and interfering with my experience of cake. The reason to strive for perfection in grammar—which I take broadly to mean the ways in which words are tied together to transmit meaning from the writer's mind to the reader's, including the ways of indicating what the "chunks" are and where they start and stop—is that errors wrench the reader's attention from the meaning and constrain it to focus instead on the smaller elements that were never meant to show. Such wrenching is frustrating; such errors are potholes in the highway of meaning, noise interrupting information. Grammar, then, is not to be seen as part of the content. When it shows, it's almost always part of the *discontent*. So, to answer your question, I want to concern myself most with content and originality, *and I will automatically do so unless I'm forced to pay attention to something else.*

Punctuation

What does it mean to achieve mastery of punctuation, and how should one set about it? If you are expecting at this point a long discussion of rules and usages, do's and don't's, why's and wherefore's—would you accept a short one instead? You probably already own a handbook, so I don't feel compelled to say everything here. Mastery of punctuation means the ability to show without ambiguity what the parts of a written thought are and how they relate to each other and to the whole. In addition, punctuation is a way for a writer to express the "personality" of his or her particular way of thinking, of joining ideas. One's punctuational idiosyncrasies are, in short, part of one's *style*. To break or bend the rules, however, you need first to know what they are. Your instructor may not wait for you to inquire about the ones that he or she considers absolute and inviolable, but if those rules are *not* provided, ask, and then review the appropriate sections in a handbook. When *I* am asked about punctuation, I begin by discussing the semicolon.

The Semicolon

You are perhaps familiar with the error known as a "comma splice." This hasty marriage of two independent clauses occurs so frequently that English instructors may consider it an act proceeding from either unshakable ignorance or simple perversity. Neither of those explanations is satisfactory. I for one believe that the comma splice is not (this is going to sound silly at first) a *comma* error at all, but that it results from people having been scared away from semicolons. The invariable answer to my question "What have you learned about semicolons?" is "I practically never use them." (One student gives this answer aloud; the rest of the class begin nodding heads in agreement.) If such has been your experience, then you know why you commit "comma splices": "practically never" becomes "never" (to be safe), and what else *is* there, usually, to put into a sentence between the capital letter that begins it and the period, exclamation mark, or question mark that concludes it? Mid-sentence punctuation comes to mean *comma*, period.

It's time to change the status of the semicolon. I want you to welcome it as a friend, to treat it as a mark of distinction in the two cases where it's called for.

1. Please use a semicolon to join independent elements that are closely related in such a way that the one on the right extends or completes the meaning of the one on the left. Example: "Finally Herbert ate the liver; he hated it, but hated it less than he feared his mother's displeasure." Note that I would not have been incorrect to insert a period after "liver" and begin a new sentence at "he." I chose the semicolon in order to *suspend* rather than to *halt* the reader's attention. The semicolon creates an expectation that the period doesn't. Lewis Thomas writes, "It is almost always a greater pleasure to come across a semicolon than a period. The period tells you that is that; if you didn't get all the meaning you wanted or expected, anyway you got all the writer intended to parcel out and now you have to move along. But with a semicolon there you get a pleasant little feeling of expectancy; there is more to come; read on; it will get clearer."[2]

2. Use a semicolon in a series of related clauses or phrases that contain commas. Example: "First

Herbert sniffed the liver, which made him ill; then, holding his nose with his left thumb and index finger, he took a bite, closed his eyes, and pretended to chew; at last he said, 'Mother, forgive me, but I won't eat it!' " If the preceding semicolons were replaced by commas, a reader would not immediately know where to pause just a little and where to pause a little more. My sentence has *three* main divisions, clearly punctuated by semicolons—not *eleven*, as it would appear to have if commas alone were used.

This second usage also applies to any series which contains items that have commas within them. For example, "Herbert invited three people to his dinner party: George, his college roommate; Sylvia, George's girlfriend; and Sally, Sylvia's cousin."

The Colon

A colon is a kind of equals sign: it tells you that what you are about to read is a restatement or unfolding of what you have just read or is in some way equivalent to it. A subtler use of the colon is to indicate that the words to the right in some sense *follow from* the words to the left: they may explain, amplify, or provide examples. The preceding sentence was one example; here are three more:

Herbert saw the first three items on the shopping list: petunias, pickles, and paper clips. (restatement by specifying the three items)

The results of the poll were not startling: the whole family, including Mother, hated the liver. (explanation by specifying the poll's results)

Three days later Herbert discovered that the unsa-
vory food was about to reappear on the dinner table:
he saw a piece of liver defrosting in the refrigerator.
(explanation of how he made his discovery)

For me, the colon is a bolder, "louder" mark
than a semicolon. When I use a colon, I can imagine hearing a trumpet fanfare; if I can't imagine a
fanfare, as in this sentence, I use the "quieter"
semicolon. Example: "Sally was everything
Herbert wanted: (da-da-da-*dum*-da-*dum*!) she was
intelligent, beautiful, healthy, young, rich, and
crazy about him."

EXERCISES

1. Could I have used a semicolon instead of a colon in
   the first sentence under the heading "The Colon"?
   Why or why not? If I could have, why didn't I?
2. Pay attention to semicolons and colons as you read,
   notice the functions they perform, and bring to class
   for discussion some examples of sentences that you
   particularly like and that would lose their charm or
   bite or precision without one or both of these marks.
3. Explain the proper way to punctuate this sentence:
   "I decided that for one day I was going to attempt the
   impossible, I would not talk for an entire twenty-
   four hour period."

The Comma

Sometimes putting in or not putting in a comma
makes little or no difference. For example, some
authors use a comma before *and* in phrases like
"Eat, drink, and be merry," and others don't. In
the construction cited, no ambiguity enters when
the second comma exits. Other times, however, a

comma before *and* is necessary because its absence renders the sentence absurd: "Herbert ate peas, potatoes, liver and peaches with cream." *Liver and peaches* with cream? Doubtful. Therefore, insert a comma after *liver*. It is always safe to put in a comma before the *and* in such cases, and to avoid the possibility of confusion, I recommend that you use it consistently.

How many commas should a sentence have? Just enough to permit a reader unambiguously to predict what's coming next. The rules for comma placement have precisely that goal. For example, we are to use commas

1. To set off introductory prepositional phrases. That's a sensible rule. Consider this sentence: "In short, pants are being worn by women as much as by men." Remove the comma, and the first three words become *In short pants*—not what the writer intends.
2. To set off names in direct address, as in "I believe, Sally, that Herbert is hungry." Without the commas, I would appear to *believe Sally about* Herbert's hunger, when what I'm doing is *informing her of* it.
3. To set off parenthetical elements. Commas around such elements, like the one you are now reading, prevent the reader from seeing the preposition *like* as a verb governed by *elements*.
4. To separate main or independent clauses. This also prevents ambiguity. Remove the comma from "Herbert loved the meal, and Sally did too," and you get the impression, temporarily, that Herbert loved *the meal and Sally*. Perhaps he does, but that's not the issue here. Remember to place the separating comma *before* the coordinating conjunction (*and, but, or, nor, for, yet*, or *so*).

5. To separate dependent clauses from main clauses in order to show where the introductory element ends. "If you don't eat the liver, you will get no dessert." Without the comma, the object of *eat* appears to be *the liver you will get*, which it is not.

A Special Comma Case: Restrictive and Nonrestrictive Clauses

Here is a well-known proverb: "People who live in glass houses shouldn't throw stones." Here, in exactly the same words, is an absurdity and a falsehood: "People, who live in glass houses, shouldn't throw stones." In the original proverb, the clause "who live in glass houses" is used as an adjective to modify *people*, informing us of the particular subset of our species that should refrain from hurling such missiles. That clause is called *restrictive* because the information it provides is essential in defining and limiting the subject. In other words, the clause *restricts* the subject by becoming part of it. *Who* shouldn't throw stones? *People who live in glass houses*. When I insert commas, however, the clause becomes *nonrestrictive*, a "by the way" clause, which asserts that (without restriction, all) people, who (by the way) live in glass houses, shouldn't throw stones. Ridiculous.

So, use no commas to set off a restrictive clause, but do use commas to signal a clause that is nonrestrictive. And when the clause refers to something other than a person or people, use *that* or *which* to introduce a restrictive clause (many instructors prefer *that*), and use , *which* to introduce a nonrestrictive clause. Example:

Flowers that bloom in the spring give me hayfever.

but

Lilacs, which bloom in the spring, smell so good that I almost enjoy my sniffles.

If I had written, "Flowers, which bloom in the spring, give me hayfever," I would have made *two different* assertions, neither of them correct: namely, that *all* flowers bloom in the spring and that *all* flowers give me hayfever. And if I had written, "Lilacs that bloom in the spring smell so good . . . ," someone would respond, "Hey! Lilacs only *do* bloom in the spring."

EXERCISES

1. Find in your reading five sentences containing restrictive clauses and five containing nonrestrictives. Are they punctuated properly? Deliberately mispunctuate them, substituting *which* for , *which* and *who(m)* for , *who(m)*—and vice versa—and enjoy the odd statements thereby produced.
2. Read over the essay you are currently working on, and check it for restrictive and nonrestrictive clauses; then make sure the punctuation correctly prepares the reader for the meaning you intend.
3. Look up the names of punctuation marks in the *Oxford English Dictionary*, especially *period, comma, colon,* and *semicolon.* You will discover, among other things, that the terms originally referred not to *marks* of punctuation, but to shorter and longer *parts* of sentences.

Just a Few More Points

Exclamation marks. Use exclamation marks sparingly. You might even vow never to use them, then break the vow when your conscience gives you a special dispensation. These "wow"-indicators lose force in proportion to their frequency: If everything is wow-worthy, nothing is. Try to arrange your words so as to produce the emphasis you want. Read your sentence aloud. Then, if the words by themselves won't convey the appropriate surprise, shock, delight, confusion, anger, or whatever, exclaim!

Dashes.   Use dashes sparingly also. Dashes set off parts of a sentence—as do commas and parentheses—but with more urgency and abruptness. A pair of dashes—like this one—performs essentially the same function as a pair of commas or parentheses. But unlike commas, dashes (parentheses, too, by the way) may—though they need not, as here—interrupt a sentence with something that doesn't fit in grammatically. I may write, for example—do you see what I'm driving at?—the sudden, interrupting question I just did by using dashes; commas can't do that job. I hope, in closing, that you find four pairs of dashes in the space of only four sentences a bit much. Writing that is full of dashes appears to be dashed-off writing, in which the author took too little care to punctuate more selectively. Think of dashes as garnishes, not as primary punctuational ingredients.

Question marks.   Use a question mark after a question, no matter how long, and only after a question.

Quotation marks.   Remember that in America periods and commas always go *inside* quotation marks at the end of a quotation, no matter what, and that semicolons and colons always go *outside*.

Don't fret about this; it's a matter of convention, not logic, reason, or morality. In Great Britain, for instance, these four marks always go *outside*. Also, question and exclamation marks go *inside* the quotation marks when what is quoted is already a question or an exclamation; otherwise, they go *outside*. Examples:

Herbert asked, "What did that man say?"

but

Do you believe that "humor is the best medicine"?

And

Sally said, "I won't eat the liver either, Herb, so give it to the cat!"

but

Mother, I heard Herbert talking in his sleep. He said, "Secretly, I love liver"!

Usage and the Avoidance of Carelessness

Overlook used to mean "look over"; that is, it used to be *used* that way. "Come here and overlook this treaty," Ben Franklin might have said to another American in Paris late in the eighteenth century. Today the remark would be a joke because *overlook* now means "disregard." If you want to find out how words are being used at any given time, open a dictionary published in that period. It's one thing for Humpty Dumpty to declare that a word means anything we want it to; H. D. is merely asserting the symbolic nature of language, the fact that there is no necessary connection between a set of letters (or the sounds they represent) and a certain meaning. Meaning is made by us, the people, and lexicographers simply describe what we do; after looking and listening, they report to us what we mean by the words we use, then put these meanings into their dictionaries.

To define means "to set limits to." Many words have multiple meanings—the preposition *of*, for example, has about sixty-eight—but no word's usages are without limit. So it is important to take care with usage, which usually involves looking words up to discover whether or not the person or people for whom you write are likely to agree about, say, the status of *contact* as a verb. (I hear you saying, "Then a dictionary *is* a lawbook!" No, unless you are referring to the commonsense "law" that advises you to know your audience, which involves knowing what your audience expects, accepts, and tolerates—and what it does not.)

I am about to present a short list of mistakes that you should try hard to avoid because they are, to an audience accustomed to formal English, neither expected, accepted, nor tolerated.[3] Let me offer, by way of preface, a short sermon. There are two classes of mistakes: errors of ignorance and errors of carelessness. Ignorance—not knowing—is everyone's predicament in certain areas and is usually nothing to be ashamed of. You don't know how to prove the Pythagorean theorem? A

[3]The classic works on usage are H. W. Fowler, *A Dictionary of Modern English Usage* (London: Oxford University Press, 1952), and Wilson Follett, *Modern American Usage* (New York: Warner Paperback Library, 1974). *The American Heritage Dictionary* is also an excellent, up-to-date resource.

book or a person will show you if you care to learn. You can't spell *ukulele*? Now you can. There are many pieces of knowledge that the average educated person will *not* fault us for not having. But there are certain bits that every college student will be expected to have mastered as a matter of course (or courses). Practically no one will believe that certain errors are the result of ignorance, and most readers will therefore charge someone who commits them with carelessness. The errors *may* be due to ignorance but will usually not be perceived so. The appearence of carlessness makes a bad impresion; why, it will be asked, didn't we care *more*? And, on the off chance that these mistakes *are* seen as resulting from ignorance, woe betide. "What?! Goes to school, with taxpayers' money, and *still*, after all these years, doesn't know (whatever)!" If this sermon makes sense to you, then either learn or remember, as the case may be, to avoid the following mistakes:

1. **a lot.**   The phrase *a lot*, meaning *much*, takes two words. (There *is* a single word *allot*, meaning "to apportion.")

2. **all right.**   Two words.

3. **its, it's.**   *Its* means "belonging to it"; *it's* is a contraction of "it is." A lot of people want to put an apostrophe somewhere in *its* because they think it's necessary in order to show possession. These same people, however, have no trouble with *my* or *his*, which belong to the same family, the possessive pronouns. Here they all are:

Singular	*Plural*
my	our
your	your
his, her, *its*	their

4. **their, they're, there**.   *Their* means "belonging to them"; as you see from the list above, *their* is the plural of *its*. *They're*, a contraction of "they are," is the plural of *it's*. Here is the contracted version of the present tense of *to be*:

Singular	*Plural*
I'm	we're
you're	you're
he's, she's, it's	they're

There is the opposite of here. (It's the place you never reach because once you get "there," you're "here.") *There* is also used as a so-called "empty subject," as in "There is a mongoose in my garden."

5. **then, than**.   If *there* is the place we never reach, *then* is the time that never comes because once we get there, it's "now." In other words, *then* is to *now* as *there* is to *here*. In addition to meaning "that other time, either past or future," *then* can also be used to mean "therefore," "if that's the case," "afterwards," and "next." As you see, then, *then* has to do with sequences, either of time or of cause and effect.

Than (much simpler) is used in comparisons: more *than*, less *than*, greater *than*, worse *than*, and so forth.

6. **different than, different from**.   *From* is generally preferred. *Than* is fairly common in speech, and some readers accept it in writing, especially when it is followed by a clause. If you are in doubt, ask what your instructor's standard is.

7. **like, as**.   *Like* is a preposition; *as* is a conjunction. "Herbert behaved *like* a liver hater," but "Herbert behaved *as* I thought he would." Some

readers accept *like* as a conjunction before an elliptical clause: "Sally takes to housework like Herbert to liver" (that is, as Herbert takes to liver). Again, ask what your instructor thinks.

8. **to, too**   (No trouble with *two*, right?) The extra *o* on *too* can help you remember its usages: *also* (something extra) and *excessively* (having to do with something extra). I choose not to write too much on these two.

9. **affect, effect**.   The problem here is that these two words are used both as nouns and as verbs. The confusion clears if one starts by noting that both words have as their bases a form of the Latin verb *facere* (to do *or* make), prefixed by *ad* (to *or* toward) and *ex* (from *or* out of).

Okay. As a verb, *affect* means to "do to" or "influence," as in "The heat affects my mood." *Effect* means to "produce" or "give rise to": "I wish someone would salt the clouds to effect a thunderstorm and cool things off." As a noun, *effect* means a "result," and *affect* as a noun is a technical term in psychology meaning "emotion" (compare *affection, affectionate*). One thing more: *affect* as a verb also means to "assume," to "put on," to "pretend": "Herbert affected a snobbish air as he refused the overcooked liver." I hope that this paragraph will prove effective; I'm trying to affect you so that you can effect any necessary changes in your use of these words.

10. **accept, except**.   Just like *affect, effect* (almost). The root here is *capere* (to take). To *accept* means to "include," to "receive," to "say yes to"; to *except* means to "exclude," to "reject," to "say no to." *Except*, sometimes followed by *for*, is also used as a preposition meaning *all but* or *not in-*

cluding: "Herbert can accept everything except the liver."

11. **lie, lay**. The difficulty here is only partly that *lie* is an intransitive verb and *lay* a transitive one—you can just *lie*, but you can't just *lay*; you have to lay *something*. In addition, the past tense of *lie* is . . . *lay*:

	to lie		*to lay*
present tense	lie		lay
past tense	lay ————	*trouble*	laid
past participle	lain		laid

To *lie* means either to "assume a prone position," to "be in a prone position," or just to "be," as in "How do things *lie*?" for "How *are* things?" To *lay* means to "put," "place," or "set." So, "Now I *lie* down to sleep," but "Now I *lay me* down to sleep."

12. **sit, set**. *Sit* is intransitive, and *set* is transitive. Essentially, *sit* is to *lie* as *set* is to *lay*. Fewer have trouble with the *sit/set* distinction because their principal parts (*sit, sat, sat/set, set, set*) do not overlap.

13. **disinterested, uninterested**. *Disinterested* means "impartial," "neutral," "unbiased," "objective"; *uninterested* means "not interested." Although these words might seem identical from the viewpoint of logic—same root, prefixed by a form meaning *not*—they are utterly distinct in use. A disinterested observer may be fascinated by what he or she observes.

14. **who, whom**. Although the distinction between the subject pronoun *who* and the object pronoun *whom* is beginning to vanish from the speech of even the highly educated, in formal writing the difference is still largely observed. *Who*

belongs to the I-you-he-she-it-we-you-they family, and *whom* to me-you-him-her-it-us-you-them. "Herbert is a man (*who* or *whom*?) I like." *Whom*, because you would say, "I like *him*," never "I like *he*." "Sally is a woman (*who* or *whom*?), you find, grows on you like algae." *Who*, because you would say, *"she* grows," never *"her* grows." "Herbert and Sally were ready to give the liver to (*whoever* or *whomever*?) wanted it." This is a tricky one. The preposition *to* seems to call for the object pronoun, but the answer is *whoever* because of the rule that the case of a pronoun is governed by its function in its own clause. You would say "*he* or *she* wanted it," never "*her* or *him* wanted it."

15. **agreement**.   Subjects and verbs must *agree*, and so must pronouns and their antecedents (words that come before them and to which they refer); that is, they must indicate the same *number* (singular or plural) and the same *person* (first, second, or third). That's it. So what are the problems? They tend to involve the words *everyone*, *everybody*, *anyone*, *anybody*, *none*, and a few others, which are formally and historically singular but which often seem to have a plural sense. Constructions like "Everybody does what they please" are now current in *spoken* English, and such usage is leaking more and more into writing. And in truth, almost any alternative is surrounded with difficulties. For example, "Everybody does what *he* pleases" is interpreted to be sexist; "Everybody does what *she* pleases" is, therefore, also sexist; and "Everybody does what *he/she* or *she/he* or *he or she* or *she or he* pleases" is bulky.

Many instructors recommend the traditional masculine pronoun unless the writer knows that the reader strongly prefers something else. The best advice, though it may not be entirely satisfactory, is to consider your usage carefully, taking into account the demands of both courtesy and clarity, which in some cases may seem to conflict—then make your decision and follow it consistently throughout a piece of writing. When you can, find out what usage will be received as *noise*, and avoid that usage. It is sometimes possible to solve the problem by switching to the plural when you can do so without loss of precision: "People do what they please." Another way out is to change the form of the sentence. Instead of worrying with, for example, "If someone calls, tell him or her that I'm out," you could write, "If someone calls, say that I'm out" or "If someone calls, I'm not home."

As you have surely noticed by now, I consistently use *he or she*, bulky though it is, when I can't get around the difficulty. Once I thought—and I was not the first—that we needed a whole new set of personal pronouns, sexless and disinterested, like *himmerself* for *himself or herself.* But pronouns are extraordinarily stable features of a language, and anyway new constructions are likelier to exacerbate the problem than to neutralize it.

16. **dangling participles and other modifiers**. The *-ing* form of a verb (*eating, giving, talking*) is called its *present participle*; the *past participle* is the form used to construct compound past tenses (*eaten, given, talked*). People often accidentally use participles in such a way that it is not clear who or what is doing the doing or to whom or to what the deed was done. In such cases, the participles are said to "dangle," because they are

not securely attached to what they're supposed to modify. "While eating the liver, Sally saw Herbert grimace." Who's eating the liver, Herbert or Sally? If it's Herbert, the sentence should read "Sally saw Herbert grimace as he ate the liver" or "While eating the liver, Herbert grimaced, and Sally saw him." Now, what about "Half-eaten, Herbert sneaked the liver onto his lap"? Either Herbert is being outrageously punished, or we have a dangling past participle in *eaten*. Assuming that the latter explanation is correct, we fix the sentence to read "Herbert sneaked the half-eaten liver onto his lap." Always keep modifying words and phrases as close as possible to what they modify.

17. **it's I, it's me**.   "It's I" and "It was Herbert and I who came to the party" show correct formal usage of the subject pronoun. To many, however, those sentences sound wrong. Thus I often hear utterances—always signaled by a look on the face that says, "Okay, everybody! Here comes some pretty fancy grammar!"—such as "They invited Herb and *she* to the party," or "Sally gave the cake to Herb and *I*." No. "They invited Herb and (they also invited) *her*"; "Sally gave the cake to Herb and (she also gave it to) *me*."

18. **pointless pointers**.   The demonstrative pronouns (*this, that, these,* and *those*) and the relative pronouns *(who(m), which,* and *that)* are words that *point*, and a writer must be careful to leave no doubt about what they point *to*. It's a good idea to ask yourself "This *what*? That *what*? Who's the *who*? Which is the *which*?" and so on. It's simply discourteous to offer your reader what will be taken as an unambiguous pointing signal and then make him or her behave like a lighthouse beacon trying to locate a lost ship.

Consider the following sentences. "As a confirmed carnivore, I am repeatedly offended by vegetarians who believe that theirs is the only moral way to eat and that, therefore, all people should avoid meat. This is especially evident in the United States." This *what*? This *meat*? No. This *offense*? No, for merely *believing*, a silent activity, cannot by itself be offensive. *This* must mean "militant vegetarians, whose language and actions are directed against meat-eaters." The second sentence, then, should read "These militant vegetarians are currently on the rampage in the United States."

19. **continual, continuous.** *Continual* means "regular but intermittent"; *continuous* means "going on without a break." I am continually amazed by the beauty and variety of wildflowers, but if I were continuously amazed by them, I wouldn't have time for anything else. Continuous two-block-long lines of people continually discourage me from going to see current hit films.

20. **imply, infer.** To *imply* means to "express indirectly," to "suggest"; to *infer* means to "conclude" or "perceive." An implication goes *out of* something, and an inference comes *in from* something. If I *imply* something, you may *infer* something from my implication. Herbert implied his dislike of liver when he refused to eat it; from his refusal, Herbert's mother inferred his dislike.

21. **consensus.** *Consensus*, all by itself, means "a shared opinion," "an agreement"; therefore, never use the phrase "consensus of opinion."

22. **the reason is that.** Don't write, "The reason is *because*." *Is* is an equals sign; therefore, "the reason is" must be followed by a noun, pronoun, or noun clause or phrase. *Because* is a conjunction. The reason I mention this error is that it oc-

curs so frequently. (Or, I mention this error because it occurs so frequently.) Please help to obliterate it.

Amen. Improper usage temporarily confuses the reader—who expects to get meaning easily—and produces distaste, not misunderstanding. For if a reader or listener detects an error, then he or she must have been able to comprehend what one *meant*. But proper usage gets the job done smoothly. To wire an electrical receptacle with snub-nosed pliers is possible, but it is not pleasant; with needle-nosed pliers there is a felt rightness. And anyone can open a pecan with a hammer, but a good nutcracker delivers satisfaction along with the intact, elliptical meat.

Spelling

A stoodent hoos speling lepht mach to bee dezired —namelie korecktnes—wunce ridooced a clas to tiers ov lafftor wyth tha remarck that it was "*boring* to spell a word the same way every time." I'd never heard such an amusing excuse before, nor a more fruitful one: Spelling is *supposed* to be "boring," so that a reader doesn't have to pay attention to it. The first sentence of this paragraph was difficult to read because you had to stop to figure out individual words. No one, I trust, spells as poorly as I affected to do in order to make my point, but *any* perceived misspelling will have the undesirable effect of forcing a reader's attention from meaning to words. Every time. Rite? Right. And sometimes, if words are misspelled beyond recognition, the meaning itself suffers.

Spelling is more a matter of convention than logic. In *How Children Fail*, John Holt tells of a child who burst into tears on being shown the spelling of *once*, so much did it violate his idea of how *o*'s behave. Melvil Dewey (1851–1931), inventor of the Dewey decimal classification system, considered English spelling grossly inefficient and wrote in his own shorthand, in which his name came out *Melvil Dui*. But although conventional spelling may on occasion appear inefficient, capricious, or even absurd (*once, sure*), enough people agree about it to make it a relatively stable norm.

The spelling of individual words is also more a matter of knowledge than intelligence. But intelligence can get knowledge, so the intelligent poor speller either asks a good speller to read his or her work for errors or uses the dictionary. I recommend the dictionary, which is surer and easier to keep handy. The answer to "How can I look it up if I can't spell it?" is "By diligent trial and error." Imagine that, never having seen the word, you hear "sə-roō'-lē-ən'," meaning "sky blue," and want to use it in writing. With what might it begin? The possibilities are ... EXERCISE: What? (Time how long it takes you to find the word.) You can also go for help to Joseph Kreirsky and Jordan L. Linfield's *The Bad Speller's Dictionary* (New York: Random House, 1967) and to Peter and Craig Norback's *The Misspeller's Dictionary* (New York: Quadrangle/The New York Times Book Co., 1974), which are useful for people who spell the way they hear.

Try to discover a pattern or patterns in the words you characteristically misspell. The first step is to keep a list, the second is to group any that belong together, and the third is to remember as many correct spellings as you can. Use your list as a checklist when giving your work a final proof-reading. The goal is perfection, a goal within the reach of most people. Strive toward it.

Neatness

Reading takes energy, and the less energy the reader has to use up in decoding a message, the more there is for understanding and appreciating it. Like spelling, punctuation, and usage, the physical appearance of a message should permit the reader to arrive at meaning without obstruction or distraction. *Doesn't this sentence take you longer to process and appear less authoritative than the one set in type before? And the handwriting isn't even so bad.* In fact, script or print that is too beautiful will also force a reader to notice words, if not letters, first, and meaning second. **Don't you agree?** It's difficult to pay attention simultaneously to both the physical form of a message and its meaning; aim for meaning. The neater a message is, the less *noisy*—and that's just what a writer and a reader are after. Let me suggest, then, that you learn how to type. It's a useful skill in college and beyond. When someone else types your work, you lose the chance to make last-minute corrections and improvements; it takes an exceptionally friendly typist—or a well-paid one—to do a second or third version.

Revision: Seeing Again

The writer so fortunate as to produce a perfect draft in one or more inspired sittings may find revision, the process of re-seeing or seeing again, an occasion for nothing but self-congratulation. Such cases, however, are sufficiently rare to warrant the following advice, which is based on the assumption that you will have composed, edited, and tested your first draft according to the ideas already presented, at least twenty-four hours before it's due.

1. Do something *else* for at least two or three hours, preferably longer, between completing the draft and starting to revise it. Reason: it is too easy to be unduly pleased with the sentences you have just written if you have written decently at all anywhere in the piece. On the other hand, if you have a strong sense that the thing has gone all wrong, you will be too discouraged to engage in anything but self-pity immediately after the fact. Let the mind and body be busied with another activity.

2. When you return to the draft, test it again for organization and coherence by outlining it according to the procedure at the end of chapter 2. This step may take almost no time, but if you have made substantial changes as the result of applying some ideas from chapters 3, 4, and 5, another look will assure you that the essay still holds together or show you that it needs more attention.

3. Now, unless your handwriting is *very* clear, type your draft, double-spaced, or print it on alternate lines to allow room for changes. Many rough drafts look like battlefields on which the writer

lost something, even if victory did come at last. Merely translating a piece of writing from the first-draft jumble of blots, blurs, arrows, and lines going every which way to a clear, clean array of type or print constitutes a primary revision, a see-ing not so much *again* as it is a seeing for the first time.

4. Read your essay out loud. By this I do not mean reading in a sort of muffled whisper; I mean aloud, as though you are presenting a speech. The ear is in some ways a more sensitive critic than the eye, perhaps because people have been speaking and listening to language for thousands of years longer than they have been writing and reading it. Reading aloud will highlight accidental sentence fragments, comma splices, noisy repetitions, dangling modifiers, and problems of agreement; and the more you practice, the more surely you will profitably combine eye, voice, and ear. Make the necessary changes.

5. If you have not yet shown your essay to some-one else, do so now. Have that person or those people read it both silently and aloud to you. Giving the piece to someone else provides the objectivity that you, who are still too close to it, lack. Carefully consider what you and your audience hear, and be prepared to make changes small or (gulp!) large.

6. A final point. After all the re-seeing—the re-structuring for coherence, the making of a neat copy, the reading aloud, the seeking out of objective criticism—and after all the appropriate modifications have been made as a result—you should go back over your essay and ask, "Do I *like* this? Is

it 'me'?'' Perhaps there were elements in the rough draft that were better, that more nearly said something with conviction, sincerity, and grace. Don't let these fine things go.

Chapter 6

Looking Again: A Preface to Writing the Research Paper

Opportunities and Problems

Everything I've said in earlier chapters about "regular" essays applies also to the construction and presentation of a documented paper. The one significant difference is that with the former, what you put together for yourself and your reader is primarily the result of researching the private library of your own mind, whereas with the latter, you must integrate personal knowledge and ideas with the published ("made public") private property of others.[1] Formally to give credit to your sources is at once an act of thanks to the au-

---

[1] As printing with movable type spread across Europe and the rest of the world in the early seventeenth century, authors were for the first time able, in large numbers, to earn considerable money from the sale of their works. Hence copyright laws and the new crime of *plagiarism*, the theft of a brainchild, which derives from the Latin word for *kidnapper*.

thors ("without whose diligence and insight this essay could not have been written"), a recognition of their legal rights, and a courtesy to your reader, who may wish to pursue the subject further by studying more of someone's work than you chose to cite for your particular purpose.

Your purpose.

Learning to quote, paraphrase, and document is not the ultimate purpose of the research essay but only part of the means toward it. *Yours* is the inquiry; your sources provide the support for the results of your investigation. *You* call the tune and direct the choir; they sing on cue.

The purpose of assigning a research essay should be to allow you to satisfy a specific curiosity. On the way to that goal you discover that the stored products of human thought and feeling— our collective curiosity—are both enormous and available. Detail: the closed stacks of the Library of Congress alone contain more than 350 miles of bookshelves, longer than the northern border of Pennsylvania, but more importantly marking a boundary between the state of humanity and that of all other animals. All creatures but ourselves start from scratch generation after generation. As far as they know, they have neither history nor future, and even if they can be said to progress genetically in response to changing environments, it is also true that they have no consciousness of such adaptation. Man is the animal with libraries.

Yet many students enjoy the prospect of writing a research paper about as much as they look forward to visiting the dentist. Why?

Research denotes "look again" and may be understood in two distinct ways. The right interpretation says that you wish to discover something not immediately obvious, something which puzzles or intrigues you, and you care enough about finding it so that, if you fail at first, you'll *look again*. The wrong interpretation goes like this and accounts, I imagine, for much of the trouble: Here is something that people have looked for before and either found or not found (or found and then lost); and whether you're interested or not, *you're going to look for it again*. The looking may be difficult in either case, but if you care about the project, frustrations encountered along the way will tend to challenge and stimulate when they would otherwise only make an already unpleasant task intolerable.

Another problem is that no matter what the topic, your interest and excitement may evaporate in the heat of undue emphasis on footnote and bibliographical techniques, rendering you a member of the bored. What to do?

Solutions

Finding an Interesting Topic

Because you can learn the methods of conducting and presenting research by pursuing almost anything, you should investigate something that interests you. Choose your own topic or one you're glad your instructor provides. As an aid to exploring the contents of your mind, here is a topic generator that is similar to the first heuristic device in chapter 2.

Step 1. Using words or phrases, list ten things you wonder about—for example, sources of doubt, confusion, perplexity, admiration, awe, anger, or delight.

Step 2. For each of the items in Step 1, write the question that specifies what needs to be explored.

Step 3. Now, choose the three questions from Step 2 that appeal most to your interest and curiosity, and rank them in order of attractiveness.

Step 4. For each question from Step 3, write a paragraph explaining the reasons for your interest in and curiosity about the answer.

Step 5. Figure out and write down five additional questions that grow out of each of those from Step 3.

Step 6. Seeing now, from Step 5, some ramifications of the original questions, would you rank those three questions differently? If yes, what is the new order, and why?

Step 7. Choose a "winner" from among the three candidates. Write it down again, and underneath write the subsidiary questions from Step 5, plus any others you can now think of.

Step 8. Study each of the subsidiary questions to see if any of them can be further divided. Which can, and into what?

Step 9. This is your step into the library. It is likely that you won't yet have a firm thesis because you don't yet know enough about the subject. But you do know what your questions are, and once you start to look for answers, more and better questions will occur to you.

Give this method a try. If you find yourself approaching Step 9 full of energy and enthusiasm, fine. If not, here's another method, which involves using what you read as a stimulus to "creative wondering." You can teach yourself to ask interesting questions that "spin off" from your reading by association with other things you know or wish you knew. The source of the examples that follow is an article by Anthony Brandt in the November 1977 *Atlantic* entitled "Lies, Lies, Lies." Mr. Brandt, the editor notes, is also the author of *Reality Police: The Experience of Insanity in America* (1975). To give you an idea of the article's drift, here are the first three paragraphs.

A friend of mine told me the following story about himself, and it occasioned the reflections on lying that are the subject of this essay. The story is so ordinary as to be practically a cliché, but perhaps that makes it all the better as a basis for discussion.

My friend is married, a father, and the owner of a beautiful house in the suburbs, an old house surrounded by terraced lawns and enormous maple trees. It was on one of these lawns, he said, on a lovely Sunday morning in early June, that the central action in his story occurred. He and his wife had held a large party the night before, and he had invited some friends from the city whom his wife didn't know. One of them was a woman, young, very attractive, who came and left by herself, who clearly knew him well, and whom his wife naturally regarded with mingled curiosity and suspicion. He knew that eventually his wife would challenge him for an explanation. Who was she? How did he know her? Why did he ask her to the party? He spent the evening, he said, wondering when the challenge would come and how he would respond to it. The party was so large, however, and host and hostess were so busy, that the question did not come until the next morning, when they were sitting on the grass together, in the shade of one of the trees.

The interesting part of the story is that the young woman was not my friend's mistress, to use the old-fashioned word, and he was not sure that he wanted her to be. In a sense, then, he had nothing to hide. But he clearly felt that he did. For all his success in a rather mundane business, which I had better leave unnamed, my friend has a great deal of imagination and is something of a romantic besides; and one sign of it is a tendency to see large meanings in coincidences. He had met his young woman friend in what he felt was such an extraordinary manner that he was sure it meant something equally extraordinary, something transcending the usual love affair. They had entered the same shop at the same time, each carrying the same make and model of tape recorder, each tape recorder needing repair. They both, it turned out, had to take their tape recorders to another place downtown—all of this took place in New York— and they shared a cab. Afterward they had a drink together and wound up spending three hours in a bar, talking. He said that she fathomed him—the word is his—in a way he found almost frightening; she guessed his business, his status in that business, his interest in the ideas of Carl Gustav Jung, and even his university. Before parting they exchanged phone numbers. She subsequently did some secretarial work for him, which he made up just to keep her in sight, and in a few months there developed between them what he was convinced was more than friendship, was indeed a kind of love but not at all sexual in nature, a fact, he said, it was difficult for both of them to get used to.

The first thing I wondered about was the author. (People are almost always good candidates for wondering.) Thus,

1. Who is Anthony Brandt, and why should anyone be interested in him or in what he has to say?

The word *insanity* in his book's subtitle next piqued my curiosity; I wondered

2. What does someone in Virginia (I live in Virginia) have to do to be considered insane? Compare that answer with the definition of "insanity" in one other Southern state, one Northeastern state, one Midwestern state, and one Western state. Summarize what mainly interests you, and comment appropriately. (My acronym for that last sentence, which I frequently give as a direction, is **SWMIYACA**.)

3. Are there measurable physiological differences between a sane person and an insane person? Or is insanity a purely socially defined behavioral deviance?

From "cliché" in the essay's first paragraph, I derived a question you may already have anticipated:

4. *Cliché* is a printing term. Visit a local newspaper, and find out what its clichés are. When did the word come to mean a trite, overworked phrase? Has anybody written a history or compendium of clichés? Learn what you can about all this, and reveal the most interesting information you turn up.

The word *lie* and the fact of the wife's impending challenge came together to make me wonder about lie detectors. So,

5. Who invented the lie detector, and how does it work? How accurate is it? Can someone beat it? In what cases, if any, is lie detector evidence admissible in state and federal courts?

The phrase "nothing to hide" in paragraph 3 made me wonder

6. What is the neurophysiology of lying to oneself? That is, how can the mind simultaneously believe that *X* is and is not true?

7. According to current psychological and psychiatric theory, what do people try hardest to hide from themselves, with what success, and with what effects? SWMIYACA.

8. What does Carl Gustav Jung have to say about lying to oneself or to others? How about Freud? What are the essential differences between Jungian and Freudian psychoanalysis? Are there any other major psychoanalytic theories and methods differing significantly from those two? SWMIYACA.

"Tape recorder" made me curious to ask

9. How does a tape recorder work? What is the one-to-one correlation between sounds and whatever is electrically imprinted on the tape? Who invented magnetic tape, anyhow? Was the discovery accidental or deliberate? And what's this new metal tape? What can it do that plastic tape can't?

Paragraph 4 of Brandt's essay ends with the sentence, "There was only the morning after, and the inevitable question," and although "morning after," in context, has nothing to do with overindulgence in alcohol, the phrase set off some cross-referenced memory cells—say, I wonder:

10. How is information stored and cross-referenced in our brains? Does anyone know anything about this? SWMIYACA.

As I was saying, I made the connection between "morning after" and the results of drinking too much, and wondered,

11. What exactly is an alcohol hangover? How is the body affected? When did the word *hangover* come into English, and what is its origin? Discover as many

"morning after" remedies as you can, from ancient times to the present, and comment on their supposed and actual effectiveness.

In paragraph 5, the husband lies about how he met the woman, and in paragraph 6 he is said to feel "contempt . . . because she [his wife] . . . believed him. . . . " Hmm. I recalled an adage, and asked,

12. "Familiarity," it is said, "breeds contempt." What is the origin of this statement? Does current psychological thinking tend to support or refute it?

Brandt begins paragraph 7, "The contempt he felt for his wife is not hard to understand. The criminal inevitably feels contempt for his victim; otherwise he could not do to him what he does." I wondered about that assertion, and Brandt's reasoning.

13. Does current criminal theory agree with Brandt's assertion that an offender feels contempt for a victim? What has been and is being learned about a criminal's attitude toward a victim? Who's studying this sort of thing, how, and with what results? SWMIYACA.

A few sentences later, Brandt mentions that "The forked tongue is indeed an appropriate image for it [that is, for duplicity]." I wondered,

14. Who first suggested the image of the forked tongue to represent lying, when, and in what culture? See if you can find books or articles about the iconography of lying. SWMIYACA.

In paragraph 8, Brandt notes that lying is as commonly practiced as it is officially censured. He then writes, "Moralists ever since [the Bible] have been repeating these commands. Practically every culture we know about includes a ban on lying in its best moral *policy*. But of course it is not always the best. We do not need Emily Post to tell us that if we are honest on all occasions we may gain an incredible reputation for honesty but lose every friend we may have had." These sentences are a mine for wonderings:

15. How were found-out liars treated by peers and by the law in various older societies—for example, ancient Judea, Greece, Rome, Elizabethan England? Look around and choose. What about African tribes, past or present? Colonial America? Immerse yourself in the subject, limit as you see fit, and SWMIYACA.

16. Who is (was?) Emily Post, and how did she come to be an authority on etiquette? Does she have any competition these days? What is the history and importance of etiquette books in America, England, France, Russia—anywhere you like? SWMIYACA.

17. The seventeenth-century French playwright Molière wrote *The Misanthrope*, which bears out Brandt's assertion that a totally honest person is a social misfit. How many other plays, stories, and novels have been devoted to the subject of honesty? Read a few, including Molière's play. SWMIYACA.

Well, I hope that's enough to give you an idea of how to go about wondering all over the place—that "place" being your own mind and the "how" a partly deliberate, partly unpredictable linking of what you know or imagine can be known with pieces of a text. Not all questions generated in this way will be equally interesting or fertile, and some will be too big and will require limiting. The goal is to wonder enough to find something that seems worth pursuing. You will discover that when you start looking for *answers*, you will also be able to ask better *questions*, questions you couldn't have posed earlier because you didn't know enough. And your early research may lead you on a tangent, away from what you begin with. That's fine; the important thing is to get interested and curious, to be willing to look, and look again.

On Not Getting Bogged Down in Mechanics

Your instructor will probably ask you to present your research essay in a certain standardized format of his or her own devising or to follow a certain published style manual. Or you may be asked to select your own. In any case, be consistent. If your essay concerns language, literature, or the humanities, it is appropriate to use the *MLA Handbook* (New York: The Modern Language Association, 1977). But if your topic has to do with chemistry, you are better off with the American Chemical Society's *Handbook for Authors of Papers in the Journals of the American Chemical Society* (Washington: American Chemical Society Publications, 1967). Other organizations with published style manuals include the American Psychological Association, the American Institute of Physics, the American Mathematical Society, the American Society of Mechanical Engineers, the Council of Biology Editors—and those devoted to studies in history, music, education, law, business, and economics. If you are in doubt about which to use, ask a reference or a serials librarian or a published author from the relevant academic department. Because you may do such a good job that your essay will become an article in a journal or a book, act accordingly now; it will save time later.

About saving time: remember, no matter what format you follow, your aim is to provide maximum bibliographical information with minimum fuss. Notes at the feet of pages may look elegant—with those impressive underlinings, abbreviations, numerals, and punctuation—but they are not fun (for me, anyhow) to type. I prefer endnotes, though you or your instructor may think differently. And whether the notes are foot- or end-, you may be permitted (and want) to make only as many as there are distinct sources from which you quote or paraphrase. Subsequent references can then be given parenthetically in the text of your essay, saving the reader from breaking his or her concentration only to be greeted with *Ibid.* or something equally devoid of immediate interest.[2]

For example, suppose you're writing a paper attempting to account for the perennial popularity of the sixteenth-century French essayist Montaigne and that one of your sources is Lewis Thomas's chapter "Why Montaigne Is Not a Bore" in *The Medusa and the Snail.* After the first reference, indicate a superscript:

---

[2]Substantive notes, like this one, are another matter. When you want to include something that is pertinent, but tangential or excessively detailed—a "by the way" that fits the subject but not the overall texture of your essay—put it into a note. For an extreme example of this technique, see Alexander Pope's *The Dunciad Variorum* in *The Poems of Alexander Pope*, ed. John Butt (New Haven: Yale University Press, 1963), pp. 329–426.

Ever since he wrote them, the essays of Montaigne have been widely read and appreciated, which may be taken as a pat on the back for us the readers. "It is one of the encouraging aspects of our civilization," writes Lewis Thomas, "that Montaigne has never gone out of print."[1]

Then, as your first full note, provide the citation thus:

[1]Lewis Thomas, The Medusa and the Snail: More Notes of a Biology Watcher (New York: The Viking Press, 1979), p. 146.

In case you refer to this source again, you can do so as follows in the text:

One great pleasure of reading is that occasionally we find authors who seem to be writing directly to us, personally.   Montaigne is one such author. He "makes friends in the first few pages of the book, and he becomes the best and closest of all your friends as the essays move along.   To be sure, he does go on and on about himself, but that self turns out to be the reader's self as well" (Thomas, pp. 147-48).

Should you provide a bibliography at the end of your research essay? Probably. When I was an undergraduate, I thought it was silly to add one, for all the documentation was already there in the notes. It was a trick to make me learn another way to play with punctuation and to test my virtuosity as an alphabetizer and typist! Then one day I realized that such a list, besides making it convenient to show sources from which I had profited but from which I had not quoted or paraphrased, was fundamentally a kindness to the reader, giving in one easily copyable place all the information needed to begin digging deeper. I now divide my own bibliographies into "List of Works Cited" and "List of Works Consulted"; your instructor may prefer something else, and so may you.

A final suggestion: When you take notes on a source, be sure to copy down *all* bibliographical information whether you think you'll use the source or not, as well as the call number, in case you have to recheck something later. Be certain to set off quoted material in quotation marks and to mark the page number for each quotation and paraphrase. It's better to be safe than to scurry to the library at 3:00 A.M. the night before your essay is due, especially as the building may be closed.

The Library

Librarians, in my experience, are helpful, friendly, courteous, kind, cheerful, and brave. I purposely use these terms from the Boy Scout Oath because a librarian *is* a scout, a highly trained and certified whiz at Finding It. It is simply not true that librarians are stodgy folk with right forefingers welded perpendicular to their lips, whose chief desire is to keep books from contamination by being read or (horrors!) removed from the premises. If anything, library personnel complain that the wealth of resources they oversee is not used enough.

The one thing you need to know immediately about your library is the location of the reference desk. Now I am aware that just as all of mankind can be divided into those who stop at gas stations for directions when they're lost and those who consider such behavior "unsporting," so library patrons fall into the "askers" and the "wanderers." Be both. First, take an hour to browse in the reference section or sections. You will be amazed at the amount and variety of information that so many have spent their lives assembling. But unless your time is unlimited, *ask* how to use the major research tools, the catalogs and indexes to periodicals and abstracts. Find out about interlibrary loans, which make available to you the resources of other collections near and far. Inquire about computer searches. Finally, if your institution offers a course in using the library, try to fit it into your schedule.

Index